Stop Telling...

Start Leading!

The Art of Managing People by Asking Questions

By Frank D. Kanu

Genius One, Inc.

Stop Telling... Start Leading!

The Art of Managing People by Asking Questions

Copyright © 2005 by Frank D. Kanu

Published by Genius One, Inc.

Charlottesville, VA

http://www.GeniusOne.com

Edited by George A. Milite

ISBN-0-9774056-1-3

Library of Congress Control Number: 2004012345

To my dear and loving wife Ada, without whom I would never have written any book.

To my children Harry, Hanna and Henry who missed more dad time—every day.

To my boys René and Christian.

To Linda Leiter—a very special friend.

And last but not least to my parents.

Table of Contents

Acknowledgements

My sincere appreciation goes to everyone who has helped with this book. I couldn't have done it without them. A few stand out: Tony Hilbourne, Steve Higgins, Rainer Mohr, Harry Schmidt, Gunnar Skeid, Rod Sloane, Bill Stewart, and Richard White.

My editor George A. Milite for his outstanding editing and his professionalism.

And Ada Kanu, my partner in marriage, business and life. I would be lost without her.

Foreword

Frank D. Kanu is the personification of the American international manager. Highly intelligent and experienced in the field of international business, he is very aware of the promise business has of bringing people closer together in the process of fulfilling the business needs of peace and understanding.

With this book, Kanu shows that managers need more than the predefined answers in daily business dealings and demonstrates how any leader can use a logical, step-by-step process to create and implement a powerful new sense of direction in his or her own organization, based on the Socratic Tradition.

Why should managers use the Socratic Method instead of simply telling employees what to do or giving them direction? What would your reaction be if you were in a situation where you had a tough challenge, or needed a clear answer to a business problem and someone just walked up to you and told you the answer? I am sure that you would feel that you have been deprived and would be annoyed and discouraged. Giving someone the answer to a problem or question is robbing them of valuable educational opportunities, because in each of us, learning happens much faster when we solve managerial problems ourselves; and when we figure something out for ourselves, we are enthusiastic to go make it happen. In this book, Kanu shows in a most effective manner how a versatile manager can become a more creative leader who does not deprive people of the joy and energy of discovery, but rather helps them to move forward by asking Socratic questions. Managers and leaders at all levels can use these proven techniques, including planning, communication, and motivational tools, to support their employees in effecting the positive changes that will make the difference in achieving their organizations' bottom-line goals. The definitional method of Socrates is a real contribution to the logic of philosophical inquiry. It inspired the dialectical method of Plato and exerted a considerable influence on the logic of Aristotle. Readers will find this book to be an invaluable resource to which they will often return to, to revise Frank D. Kanu's practical advice as their business grows to meet the worldwide markets of the 21st Century.

Dr. Jay-D Olivier
Professor - International Business Law
Amsterdam and London

Introduction

Flashback: a warm summer night, almost twenty years ago. My best friend—financial director of a European trust—and I were drinking coffee and philosophizing about business. At one point he makes a statement that changes the mood and makes me pause: "People are born either as managers or as worker bees."

Wow!

Is my friend right? Do you really have to be born a manager, or leader? Is it true that some of those skills can never be learned?

> *"Management is nothing more than motivating*
> *other people."*
> *Lee Iacocca*

"I can do that!" many will answer. "I can motivate others." But how? In 2004 Henry Mintzberg famously asked for "managers, not MBAs" in his book of the same name. In May 2005 the *Harvard Business Review* published "How Business Schools Lost Their Way," Warren Bennis' and James O'Toole's take on managers failing because of the theoretical-centered education provided by most top business schools.

Is there really anything new? Can any management guru teach you something that hasn't yet been discovered and put into practice?

No.

In fact, when you encounter "experts" who claim they've discovered something new, my advice is, run! The truth is that it's all about existing knowledge presented in new ways. More than that, it's about teaching knowledge in ways the student understands—and uses.

Everyone who teaches—and managers should teach their employees—ought to be able to recognize quickly how well the student is taking in the material being taught, and how to adjust the flow of information to each student's needs. Among the essential components for a successful teaching experience are high standards and expectations, ongoing feedback, and a dynamic that engages both teacher and student. The problem is that too often the *process* becomes the focus instead of the *results*. How often have you watched a film touted as an action movie and thought "Come on—where's the action they promised?"

1. In today's fast-moving world, managers have to stay on top of the game constantly if they want to remain an asset to the company. Not only that, they have to learn how to use a wider and more complex array of tools. Having so many tools is actually an improvement; remember the old adage, "If all you have is a hammer, everything looks like a nail." But it's up to the manager to choose the best tool to meet each specific situation.

2. A successful manager will offer employees the support, encouragement, and resources necessary to get the job done. No true manager wants to be a puppet master. Support and encouragement are also important elements of implementing change. The successful manager understands that change works when the employees get positive reinforcement along with the proper tools.

3. The manager's primary duty is to strike a balance between the goals of the business and the expectations of the employees. We all know managers who only live on one side of the rope—hardliners who figuratively walk over bodies when it's to their advantage, or sympathizers who listen to every side of an argument but who fail to set goals based on what they're hearing. One-dimensional managers like these almost never win the confidence or respect of their employees.

Manager or leader? There is a great difference between the ordinary manager and the leader. Managers usually live by the rules made by others. Leaders make the rules.

Leaders will build up employees and help them grow, giving them real opportunities to one day become leaders themselves. They understand that those following them are not after their job. Leaders motivate, and they listen, so they know what their employees want and the tools they need to get the job done. Leaders also know how to balance between giving employees help and allowing them to make their own decisions.

Questions

In the fifth century B.C. the Greek philosopher Socrates perfected a method of teaching in which he would ask disarmingly simple questions that actually forced people to admit what they *didn't* know. As you read this book, you'll find a number of questions that follow the Socratic tradition. The reason? Today's managers need more than the predefined answers we might think are correct, but which seldom fit the problem at hand.

Stop Telling... Start Leading is a work book and should be used as such. It offers many open-ended questions to the manager, offering ways to determine why something has gone off-center. Because every manager is different—the result of education, cultural background, ethnicity, etc.—offering predefined "one size fits all" answers can't do it any longer. Managers need to answer tough, pointed questions that will force them to come to terms with their goals. Once they do that, they can manage more effectively and more positively—which helps them and their team.

Many management books are written with the manager as the sole reader in mind. This book will also help interested team members to better understand how and why their team works the way it does.

It will be a useful tool for all managers who see the need to implement changes in their business. Don't expect solutions or well-defined answers to every question here. Sometimes managers need to be able to refine their own solutions to find their way. Many of these questions will serve to guide managers toward that goal.

Misplaced fear. Some managers fear that implementing any new management strategy will result in a team of matching personalities—all alike, with no dynamism. There's no need to worry about that. To begin with, it shouldn't be your goal to change the people you work with; rather, you want to help them implement changes that will motivate and encourage them.

Remember that managers need to know not only that there are more tools than just one or two, but also where to find and how to use them.

More than that, they need to understand that learning and teaching is always a two-way street. If you teach without learning you do not teach. If you learn without teaching you do not learn. Managers and employees have a responsibility to each other as well as to themselves.

> *"The people who get on in this world are the ones*
> *who get up and look for the circumstances they*
> *want and, if they can't find them, make them."*
> George Bernard Shaw

This book is divided into seven steps:

Step 1: What Is Management?

Without the proper foundation, any building will be unable to stand solidly. Different existing definitions are introduced, including the classics from Maccoby, Myers-Briggs and Keirsey, as well as some lesser-known ones.

Step 2: Know the Sins

As a manager you must be well aware of the shortfalls that can break your business: starting with the 13 most deadly sins like "Demand and Encourage," "Ignore Standards," "Tolerate Negligence" or "Let Everything Go Uncontrolled." You'll learn about a manager who punished underperforming employees with a whip.

Step 3: Take Responsibility

Managers need to understand that taking responsibility means standing up for their employees. But employees need to take responsibility as well. Responsibility is more than just focusing on making money. Companies that understand the importance of customers and employees and treat them accordingly, easily outperform those that don't.[1]

---

[1] As described from John Cotter and James Heskett, *Corporate Culture and Performance* (Free Press 1992) in their research of more then two hundred big companies over an 11-year period.

Step 4: What Do You Pay?

A bonus is worth more than a thousand words. Bonuses don't have to be cash, but they do have to be meaningful and appropriate to the job being rewarded. Think how the right bonuses could make employees more motivated and loyal.

Step 5: Make Your Team Work

Designing teams seems to be turning into a lost art. Most teams are thrown together too quickly. Just throw in a few folks with a "reputation" and the rest will work itself out—or will it? Can the underdogs outperform the stars? Shotgun teams—just like shotgun weddings, just as unhappy. Managers are proud of their accomplishments, but when things go awry do they take responsibility or blame the team?

Step 6: Change, Growth and Trust

During a speech at a Rotary Club a formerly silent member felt comfortable enough to speak up. What made him feel confident enough? Skilled managers can get the best out of their employees. Through good manners, understanding cultural differences and respecting personal space and keeping things organized (or not).

Step 7: Bring the Fun to Work

Having fun can't be a requirement, but it's a desired side effect. The fun has to be added to the work expertly or else the employees will see the fun as just more work. When managers can loosen up the staff, the workplace is more relaxed and productive. The more fun, the better employees work.

Step 1

Define!

A Single Definition?

*"What you think of yourself is much more important
than what others think of you."*
Lucius Annaeus Seneca

Does it make any sense to classify managers into different categories?
It would certainly make life easier—but the truth of course is that most
managers are a mix of several classifications, several qualities. Some of
these qualities are valuable and useful; many of those qualities comple-
ment each other and make for a strong leader. Other qualities are less
desirable—or sometimes what should be a desirable quality gets misused.
And to be honest, there are some qualities that can best be described as
out of this world.

Something else to keep in mind about classifications: definitions vary
depending on the particular management culture, not to mention economic considerations. (The better the economy, the more effusive the definitions.)

Management and Management Functions

Which developments led in practice to the irreversible separating of management functions and to the development of an own management style?

First, let's start off by defining both terms:

Management

Because no individual can effectively lead a large-scale enterprise single-handedly, the duties and tasks of management get split into several sub-tasks. Those sub-tasks will then be planned and executed within clearly defined borders from (and for) several individuals. The result is a system determined to carry out individual, social, political, economical, environmental and ethical goals. That may sound lofty, but when you think about it, this really is the core of a successful, responsible, forward-thinking business. To reach these goals, the key resources have to be found, secured, procured, processed and used in the most effective way possible.

Let's take a look at a dictionary definition of management:

"Management"—(from Latin manus agere "to lead by the hand", guidance) characterizes either the group leading an organization or the associated activities and tasks to run an organization (planning, execution, control and adjustment of measures to ensure the well being of the organization).

Management Functions

Traditional management theory tells us that the typical management functions are:
1. Planning
2. Organization
3. Employment
4. Guidance
5. Controlling

These functions are valid, and it's useful to step back and explore where they originated.

Going back in history, we can see the first stirrings of what we call management quite early. Such enormous projects as the building of the pyramids or the construction of the Roman aqueducts required workers of varying degrees of skills to supply the actual labor. That labor was overseen by people who ensured that productivity was high.

The gains made in "management" in ancient Europe and Asia were countered by setbacks during the Middle Ages. There were no societies like the Roman or Egyptian empires to oversee the creation or completion of great undertakings. The economy was more centered on individual activity.

Until relatively recently, in fact, production was primarily a local activity; craftspeople and artisans produced goods on a small scale. The individual owner/artisan completely controlled production—manufacturing, selling, repairing, and creating new products. Various aspects of the production process might be delegated, usually to family members. Artisans trained others to produce by taking on apprentices; often, apprenticeships were handed down from generation to generation in the same family. The artisan served as a sort of "guidance worker" to the apprentice.

Are there "guidance workers" in your company?

Beginning in the late 18th century, when social, political, economic, and technological changes heralded the Industrial Revolution, the concept of management as we know it today started taking shape. The Industrial Revolution spurred on the now common practice of division of labor, thanks in part to the invention of machines that could do the most onerous and time-consuming tasks. As a result, workers became specialized, often in single, simple and easy-to-learn tasks. This increased the distance between the apprentice and the guidance worker. One negative side effect of this was that the individual worker lost the opportunity to be involved with the complete production process. This created the need for more experienced workers (often who had been given the more traditional apprenticeship training) to lead and oversee the production. A positive side effect of this arrangement was that production increased, sometimes dramatically. The combination of increased mechanization and increased capacity to produce meant that more raw materials were needed (never mind the new machines). The results? Manufacturers needed more capital. Because the volume of capital was so much larger, it became clear that people would be needed to manage the financial aspects of the business. Eventually, management became an essential component in planning, organization, and controlling.

In many countries the bureaucracy had (and still has) a strong influence on the development of systematic management in developing large-scale enterprises. To their credit, bureaucracies can ease the expansion of the enterprises and also ensure the economic growth of the country. One could say that bureaucracies act as "owners" just as in traditional companies, and as such they need managers to keep things running efficiently.

As the relationship between "owners" and "managers" emerged, forward-thinking owners realized that they needed to find managers. At first, they looked to the family for their leaders (many companies still do this to varying degrees), but it became increasingly clear that the best way to succeed was to hire the *most competent people to do the job*.

To manage

1. *take responsibility*
2. *lead, be in charge*
3. *observe and direct*
4. *supervise*
5. *execute*
6. *negotiate*

Do you manage—by this definition?

There are three main classifications to better understand what a manager does:

1. Intrapersonal

Representative	Supervisor	Connector[2]

2. Informational

Receiver	Sender	Speaker

3. Decision Maker

Innovator	Peace Maker	Administrator

Managers shouldn't think they need to be able to mold their personality to accommodate all of these traits or qualities. Smart managers, in

---

[2] Malcolm Gladwell, *The Tipping Point: How Little Things Can Make a Big Difference* (Back Bay Books, 2002)

fact, know that they can overcome their own weaknesses—sometimes by working on themselves, other times by delegating to people they trust. Managers, who think they're perfect, or even close to perfect, can be dangerous.

Can you name your five biggest strengths?

Can you name your five biggest weaknesses?

Short and Sweet?

Smart and Lazy

You may have heard the story of the plant manager who was asked his secret to success. "When there's a tough job, I get a lazy person to do it," he explained. "The lazy person will find the easiest and fastest way to get the job done." Smart and lazy employees are good at finding new and efficient ways to solve problems. They only go above and beyond when there's an absolute need to act. (Sometimes this is a plus; as smart and lazy people won't get caught up in minor problems.) When they do need to act, they think, plan, and execute quite effectively. Not surprisingly, they're also good at delegating. These people tend not to move beyond middle management in the organization. In part, they don't exhibit the necessary ambition, but also because top management sees them as too valuable to lose.

If they're good at what they do, why offer them challenges or a chance to grow?

Who in your team is smart and lazy?

Smart and Diligent

In his book *On War*, the German military leader Karl von Clausewitz (1780-1831) describes these managers very well[3]. They tend to be specialists and experts. Irreplaceable—especially when your companies' main business is research and development.

Who in your team is smart and diligent?

Are they working in research and development?

Dense and Diligent

These are the worker bees. They execute everything according to plan—no matter the costs. Rules and standards are important and will always be followed religiously. They may be valuable for certain tasks and they're always willing to work harder. But they lack (or seem to lack) the creativity needed to solve complex problems, or the understanding to know when to ignore the rules and standards.

Who in your team is dense and diligent?

---

[3] Clausewitz became famous although he died before completing *On War*—one of the most influential military and economical writings. Way too often it is not obvious that an idea originated from him. For example the Win-Win principle is an economical use of Clausewitz's alliance theory.

Among the better known readers of *On War* is Henry Kissinger. It was translated into innumerable languages, making it one of the most widely known books on Earth. Read at most military schools and also in many management schools like Harvard.

Does your company need worker bees?

Dense and Lazy

You have to tell them what to do—and that's exactly what they do. No more, no less. An imprecise explanation will lead to mistakes. You will find them all over the place, but (not surprisingly) you rarely see them in higher management.

Who in your team is dense and lazy?

Only Two?

Management always happens between the two extremes of vision and details. The manager has to find the right point of balance between the two. Only those managers able to find the right balance run a striving business; probably one of the darkest definitions you will come across.

The Bean Counter

The bean counter lives for details, to the point that details are split further into more details. Every single detail then gets painstakingly analyzed, often to find ways to change them. When those details are changed, they lead to more details, which leads to more analysis—and still more details and analysis. They can be relentless in their drive to change details (a never-ending cycle).

Engineers at a company that manufactures refrigerators found a way to produce the doors faster, thus saving a few minutes per door. In a large operation, of course, those few minutes add up to big gains. They proudly presented their discovery to top management, but the financial director became quite upset with the report. As he saw it, these savings in one area led to a slowdown in another. It was a stoppage of less than a second, but the financial director saw it as a waste of time and money. Thus, instead of thanking the engineers for their cost-saving idea, he instead found fault with a relatively insignificant issue.

Bean counters are hardly ever able to create a short, quick analysis of a situation. When they rise to the level of management, their need for more and more details becomes increasingly problematic, not to mention demoralizing to employees who are told their performance is never good enough.

Are you detail driven?

Or someone in the team?

Can it be changed?

Should it be changed?

The Generalist

Generalists can be as stifling to the business as the bean counters, albeit for different reasons. You can easily recognize them by their drive and vision. The trouble is that their drive and vision often comes without any tangible proof of concept. Generalists usually refuse to deal with the theory because they lack the underlying know-how. They don't want to bother themselves with proving the value of their vision—they just want to force that vision onto others.

To their credit, generalists are easier to work with than bean counters—but only to a point. They may not want a constant stream of detail and analysis—but because they have *no* frame of reference they often ask employees to complete unrealistic or even contradictory tasks. General-ists seem more easygoing because they have no concrete strategy; often they seem more like prophets than managers. Many generalists think of themselves as builders. In the end, however, generalists offer little more than castles in the air.

How many air castles have you come across?

Classics

Maccoby

Michael Maccoby,[4] a psychoanalyst who studied under Erich Fromm, came up with some of the most interesting definitions:
1. Expert
2. Helper
3. Defender
4. Innovator
5. Self developer[5]

But probably the definition with the broadest impact is "The Gamesman".[6]

Maccoby distinguishes four different types of managers:
1. The Craftsman

---

[4] Dr. Michael Maccoby is a psychoanalyst and anthropologist who consults to businesses, governments and unions on leadership and strategic development. He is president of the Maccoby Group in Washington, D.C. and has a PhD from Harvard University, where he directed the Program on Technology, Public Policy and Human Development from 1978-90.

[5] Michael Maccoby, *Why Work? Motivating the New Workforce* (Miles River Press, 1995)

[6] Michael Maccoby, *The Gamesman: The New Corporate Leaders* (Simon and Schuster, 1976)

2. The Organizational Man
3. The Jungle Fighter
4. The Gamesman

No person will be just solely one type but rather a mix of all with the main type depending on the manager's personality and the environment. Maccoby goes on to describe each of the types and how they influence a business.

And then there are the Myers-Briggs Types (based on the psychological studies of Carl Gustav Jung) and Keirsey Temperament (also named Temperament Sorter). Keirsey's studies are similar to Myers-Briggs (you can get more information about them at www.keirsey.com) and actually gave Myers-Briggs wider publicity. These studies and the results have led to probably the best known management type evaluations in the United States and many other countries.

Do you know your Myers-Briggs type?

Your temperament sorter?

While the results can be useful on a basic level, it's a good idea to keep them in perspective. Remember that no one fits completely into one category, no matter what the test. Too often, people try to live the results. At best, they become what the results implied they might be instead of being themselves. Personal highs and lows and feelings will always influence the outcomes of tests. As do heritage and education.

1. **E-I: Extrovert vs. Introvert**
    Extroverts love to connect and act quickly while introverts are more reflective and intense.
2. **T-F: Thinking vs. Feeling**
    The thinker tries to optimize decisions by applying logic and being objective. The feeler is driven by emotions, taking relationships into consideration.
3. **S-N: Sensing vs. Intuition**

The sensing person is detail-oriented and looks at the data at hand. The intuitionist depends on intuitions and tends to be a generalist.

4. **J-P: Judging vs. Perceiving**
    The judging personality will make a decision and stick to it even before all the facts are known. The perceiver relies on changing variables and will alter decisions accordingly.

Myers-Briggs Personality Type

Dominant Introverted Types

1. Intuition	INTJ & INFJ
2. Sensing	ISTJ & ISFJ
3. Thinking	INTP & ISTP
4. Feeling	INFP & ISFP

Dominant Extroverted Types

1. Intuition	ENTP & ENFP
2. Sensing	ESTP & ESFP
3. Thinking	ENTJ & ESTJ
4. Feeling	ENFJ & ESFJ

Keirsey Temperament

Dominant Introverted Types

1. Intuition	Mastermind Rational (iNTj) & Counselor Idealist (iNFj)
2. Sensing	Inspector (iStJ) & Protector Guardian (iSfJ)
3. Thinking	Architect Rational (iNTp) & Crafter Artisan (iStP)
4. Feeling	Healer Idealist (iNFp) & Composer Artisan (iSfP)

Dominant Extroverted Types

1. Intuition   Inventor Rational (eNTp) & Champion Idealist (eNFp)
2. Sensing   Promoter Artisan (eStP) & Performer Artisan (eSfP)
3. Thinking   Field Marshal Rational (eNTj) & Supervisor (eStJ)
4. Feeling   Teacher Idealist (eNFj) & Provider Guardian (eSfJ)

To Summarize:

When businesses increase in size, whether by geographical expansion, diversification, or vertical integration, it is essential that they place a strong emphasis on coordination. When there's no coordination, workflow and productivity suffer. To be able to pursue the company vision, management must coordinate if it wants to plan out and distribute the resulting work meaningfully. The management functions as defined above.

Manager = Entrepreneur?

Is a manager an entrepreneur?

Many entrepreneurs are managers, but fewer managers are entrepreneurs. One reason for this is that managers as a rule have no tangible stake in their business. A manager does not even have to own shares of the business in question. Interestingly, we all know people who are thought of as a good entrepreneur but a bad manager, but we don't hear as often of people who are considered a good manager but a bad entrepreneur.

Universities produce many MBAs. How many of them become successful entrepreneurs? True, they've learned the basics: accounting, controlling, marketing, and management. Those basics are important for entrepreneurs, too, but entrepreneurs have to bring way more to the table. In many ways the lot of the entrepreneur parallels that of the "struggling artist."

Entrepreneurs must be creative and innovative, but they also have to be inspirational. *As long as managers do not see themselves also as entrepreneurs they will not develop their full potential.* Going a step further, the responsibility of the manager is to train their team members to become managers themselves. The best performing teams are those where people see themselves as entrepreneurs within the team, not just worker bees.

Step back, relax, and look at the situation. Can you find your solution?

"Know Thyself"
Encryption over the main entrance of the Oracle of Delphi

Although entrepreneurs and managers share many traits, they also have some notable differences. Entrepreneurs are known for taking risks and thinking primarily of the long term; managers are more detail-oriented and cautious, and they do care about the short term as well as the future. Entrepreneurs believe that failure in one venture is a learning experience that will give them more momentum next time; managers are much more fearful of failure and how it will affect their reputation.

As the business world becomes more global (in part thanks to the Internet), the pressures and expectations on businesses grow. In this more competitive environment, businesses feel a need to make bolder, more long-ranging decisions. So, sometimes managers are forced to take the role of the entrepreneur.

What impact has modern society on entrepreneurship?

Can you define the entrepreneurial process?

What are the challenges an entrepreneur faces in your company; your line of business?

Do you see yourself as entrepreneur, manager or both?

Viewing shareholder value as the business's number one priority does little to encourage entrepreneurial spirit. Likewise, the many committees, boards, and regulations that come with them can squash entrepreneurship pretty easily. One of the hallmarks of successful entrepreneurship is the ability to make decisions quickly. Anything that hinders the ability to do that endangers the entrepreneurial spirit.

Managers need to understand that adopting an entrepreneurial mindset alone isn't what's needed to make the business successful. What entrepreneurship can do is unlock the visionary ideas that can give the business a boost both short- and long-term. Don't think of the entrepreneur as someone who creates chaos that managers need to fix. Think instead of that "chaos" as a vision—and use that vision to break out of the old ideas that keep the business from moving forward.

How long does it take to get a decision?

How many ideas get shut down?

Are You Managed?

Let's look at things from the point of view of an employee for a moment. (As a manager, this is directly relevant, since you're an employee, too.) Think of the job interview. Traditionally, the employer asks questions and the prospective employee dutifully answers them. Even when they're given the opportunity to ask their own questions, job-seekers seldom do. If you're in this situation but you fail to ask questions, how can you really find out whether the company you may be working for is well-managed or chaotic? (The employer's questions aren't likely to give that information away.) Job seekers are trained and counseled to answer questions, but maybe it would be better if we encouraged them to ask questions and gave them some guidance on how to do it effectively. It might keep a lot of people from stepping into the "perfect job" that ultimately doesn't turn out to be perfect at all!

> *"Good management is the art of making problems*
> *so interesting and their solutions so constructive*
> *that everyone wants to get to work and deal with*
> *them".*
> *Paul Hawken*

Are the problems interesting or boring?

Who is in charge?

Are you managed by a woman or by a man?

Does it make a difference?

Should it?

It is sad and shameful that in this day and age gender still plays a role in the business world. Words like *"smart"*, *"creative"*, *"assertive"*, and *"talented"* are neither female nor male. Yet it still happens too frequently that a woman reaches a certain rung on the management ladder but then goes no further. By keeping women from rising to their full potential, companies are eliminating half (perhaps more than half) of their talented managers suitable for the job.

Ethics and Leadership?

Ethics and leadership both seem to be abstract and ambiguous—so imagine what happens when we discuss *ethical leadership*. Ethical leadership is not about how to lead to reach specific goals, but what ethical affects leadership has. Ethics aren't morals themselves but the meaning of moral ways and actions. Ethics don't decide, nor do they take decisions away. They serve as a means of guidance—to find answers, make decisions, and know how to justify them.

Leadership is about those who are in a position to make decisions; create opinions and attitudes. It is more then just managing. Because leaders have to lead by example, their words, actions, and values play a huge role in their success. Responsibility and credibility are two of the most important elements of leadership; each is deeply based on the interaction with others. Because every action, even the smallest, has an impact, ethics are always part of the decision-making process. Ethics are not a cookbook for great decisions. Leaders know that every decision has to be carried by responsibility and credibility. To be recognized as a leader requires exuding trust. Remember that for many the values and ethics of the leader have to match their own understanding of those.

To understand the impact of ethics, it's important to ask the right questions:

1. How do we implement corporate social responsibility?
2. How do we select and support employees while achieving the business goals?

3. What core competencies does a business need to stay success-ful? How do those bind the people?
4. What values do managers need to keep the worth, responsibility and future compatibility of the business?

Today's leaders have to understand what is needed tomorrow if they want to implement the necessary changes to keep the business running. Successful leaders are smart, responsible, and ethical. They're expected to:

1. Take responsibility and delegate.
2. Continuously work on the vision and goals of the business and follow those.
3. Support shareholders, stakeholders, and suppliers to help them grow and stay within the vision and goals of the business.
4. Implement valuable, clear and responsible business solutions, either with or without the team.
5. Design smart teams with responsible team players.
6. Support employees to be themselves by bringing back the fun, and understanding diversity.
7. Change the rules (when necessary).

How much can a leader learn by looking at those who have chosen to be unethical?

If you look only at the mistakes others made without trying to under-stand why they happened, you will learn almost nothing. It may be hard to believe, but often those who behave unethically think of themselves as perfectly ethical and responsible. It's a matter of how they interpret values. They may be wrong, but remember that values do change over the years and sometimes people make errors of judgment out of ignorance rather than lack of conscience. It is a fine line to walk.

Checklist

One of the best ways you can create a set of goals for your team is to remember to follow the SMART (*Specific*, *Measurable*, *Attractive*, *Realistic*, and *Timely*) principle. Once those goals are set—they have to be evaluated constantly and adjusted when needed.

✓   *Are you in control of your own destiny?*

✓   *Is your boss?*

✓   *Are you making your own decisions?*

✓   *Are you allowed to plan?*

✓   *Can you change given plans?*

✓   *Does your word count?*

✓   *Is there too much stress and pressure?*

✓   *Are blame games part of the daily routine?*

✓   *Does money or the lack of it rule?*

✓   *Is there supervision only?*

✓   *Is the staff qualified?*

✓   *Are there teams?*

✓   *Do you feel managed?*

✓ *Does the team feel managed?*

✓ *Is the top manager representing or managing?*

✓ *Do managers in the organization follow their own words?*

✓ *Do managers meet with employees every few weeks?*

✓ *Do you like the overall feeling?*

✓ *Do you have fun?*

✓ *Are management and staff loyal? To each other and the company?*

✓ *Is everyone responsible towards customers?*

✓ *Are there entrepreneurs?*

✓ *Are there ethical standards?*

✓ *Are they followed and lived by?*

Step 2

Know The Sins!

13 Deadly Sins

"Sins cannot be undone, only forgiven."
Igor Stravinsky

Results-Oriented Instead of Goal-Oriented

Do you think you can speak of leadership if the leader has no vision, no plan?

Teams need a clear and well-defined structure. How managers manage always depends on their management style and their personality. A manager with a strong personality will leave a definitive imprint on the team. Yet even strong managers who know what they want need to make the team members feel that they are needed. One way to do this is to involve them in the management process. Make sure they know how their manager manages. Tell them the goals instead of asking for short-term results without any explanation. If you're driving somewhere you've never been before, you don't want someone to tell you to just drive north and eventually you'll get there—you want detailed directions.

Were you given a clear direction?

Can you give one?

> *"The single biggest problem in communication is*
> *the illusion that it has taken place."*
> *George Bernard Shaw*

Open the Lines of Communication

It's been said thousands of time before, but it can't be stressed enough: good communication is absolutely vital to the success of any organization. And don't think I'm talking about sending memos or talking on the phone. Communication needs to be active, personal, and ongoing. Communication within the team must be crystal clear; likewise communication between different teams.

Does everyone understand you?

Do the team members know exactly what's expected of them or have you assumed they know?

Do they communicate well with each other?

Or with you?

Managing by focusing on solving problems, and only on solving problems, is really nothing more than chaos management; don't be that short-sighted. You do want to minimize the effects of chaos, but you also have to consider the day-to-day operations that continue on even during the most chaotic conditions. Look around: even when everything seems to be going wrong, there are still things that are getting done, and getting done right. Don't let temporary chaos blind you to this.

Does chaos scare you?

What—in your opinion—counts as chaos?

Do you have goals?

And a plan and/or a vision?

How often are those reviewed?

Are they shared with the team?

Is team feedback included?

Overlook Setting Goals Together With the Employees

*"This one step - choosing a goal
and sticking to it—changes everything."*
Scott Reed

One goal of managing is inspiring your team to be the best it can be. The team members need to know the company's objectives, and those objectives have to fit with their personal and professional goals. Managers have to set clear directions to avoid confusion and to keep from becoming arbitrary in their demands. Company, professional, and personal goals should be part of the hiring process.

How often do you see management step into a problem situation, find out what's going on, and set things in motion to make the team members happy and productive? Certainly not often enough! One CEO decided that firing every employee with a bad attitude would fix the malaise in his company. In fact, he fixed nothing. Instead of taking care of the problem by trying to motivate the employees, he only battled a symptom. If the bad attitude was caused by something within the corporate culture, it's only a matter of time before other employees develop a bad attitude, too. How long will it take before the problem is back?

How often do you sit together with your team?

Is your team familiar with the company goals?

Does every team member have a plan?

Do you know where your team members want to be in a year, two years from now?

Do they know where management wants them to be?

Let Everything Go Uncontrolled

Trusting the team doesn't mean giving up control. The issue for most managers isn't whether to exert control, but how to do it.

To begin with, the team needs to demonstrate that it's worthy of trust. That comes not only from the team's actions, but the interactions between the team and the manager. If you don't know what your employees are doing—and if they don't know what you want them to do—how can you develop trust and understanding?

A team that has no one in control will likely fare worse than one that's badly controlled. Managers need to have the courage to take charge. If they do it in a spirit of shared goals with the team members, it will build mutual respect and understanding. The concept isn't really complicated. Yet think of all the managers you know who struggle to build trust and respect with the team.

Are you building trust? Respect?

Is it easy?

Drive thy business, let not that drive thee.
Benjamin Franklin

Inc. Magazine talks about workers stating that routine maintenance had been performed as part of their daily duties. During a failure of the machine it became obvious that this maintenance was never done.

When did you control the last time? If not you—who is controlling?

Are you controlling the goals you have set with the team?

What do you control?

How often do you control? Too often? Not often enough?

Do you have standard operating procedures in place for frequently reoccurring situations?

Nobody Takes Responsibility for the Team

"People think responsibility is hard to bear. It's not.
I think that sometimes it is the absence of responsi-
bility that is harder to bear. You have a great feeling
of impotence."
Henry Kissinger

Managers have different ways of dealing with people, and most employees understand that. The problem is when the manager doesn't convey a sense of responsibility for them and their jobs. Successful managers care about their staff and their achievements. Employees who don't feel that the manager cares will almost always fail to perform at their highest levels. Responsibility takes many forms. This is about how the manager comes across, not what the manager really does. Not showing that you care will cost you *and* your business.

I know of one senior manager who earned a reputation among his peers and employees as the company's most caring manager. What did he do? He let employees know that their families came first. If an employee had to take time off to stay home with a sick child, the manager didn't make that person feel guilty or less committed to the company. Instead, he would work with individuals to help them accommodate their family needs with their responsibilities on the job. The result was that the employees were more motivated because they felt an increased responsibility to the manager.

Are you forgetting that you are the boss?

Can team members come to their manager with their problems?

Do they? And if they don't—why not?

Do you take responsibility?

Demand and Encourage

How can you demand everything you can get from your team without overtaxing everyone? Too often management sets goals without considering the weaknesses and strengths of the team members. Worse still is when management sets goals for the staff that it doesn't hold itself to. Sometimes the issue can be as simple as ignoring the calendar. What do I mean by that? Consider the following instructive story.

A company botched up a huge project, partly because the project represented more work than it could handle. Or was it? The projects time line was supposed to run from November thru February—which of course includes several major holidays for a number of cultures. Employees were forced to work long hours during the holiday season, with little support from management. Why so little support? Because top managers weren't around. They had chosen that same time to take "well-deserved" vacations. We can't know whether the project could have been completed on schedule if management had been more involved, but it's hard to imagine that the staffers were feeling particularly motivated during those long hours of work.

Are goals extremely high—but still reachable?

Is know-how seen as an investment?

Does management keep the teams' morale up?

Have incentives for them?

Do you demand the best while giving the best support?

Ignore Standards

There's no shortage of standards in the business world; sometimes it seems that even standards have standards. Some people equate standards with bureaucracy, but in fact bureaucracy is more about regulations than standards. Still, standards themselves can often be cumbersome—especially when there seems to be competing standards governing the same project. Having said that, what do you suppose would happen if we had no standards at all? Worse still, what would happen if each individual employee worked according to his or her own standards?

If a company has no standards to follow, its culture will seem inconsistent from the inside as well as the outside. On the other hand, standards have to reflect the work, the culture, and the people at hand. Sometimes you need to adjust or even change standards. It's a matter of deciding when change is needed and when the status quo is the best choice. Let's face it: things change, and if you want to keep pace, you have to change, too.

> *"The quality of an individual is reflected in the standards they set for themselves".*
> *Ray Kroc*

Do you have standards?

Do you control how standards are followed?

Does the team know the standards? Are they realistic?

Are standards reviewed?

Tolerate Negligence

One employee's negligent behavior will always reflect on the whole company. By negligent I mean careless, inattentive, or somehow inappropriate to the situation. The number of consumer complaints about careless employees has increased over the years. Companies should be mindful of this because dissatisfied customers react—usually by taking their business elsewhere.

Think about how you change your shopping behavior after you've had a bad experience with an employee. Yet many companies do nothing to fix this. And don't think negligence is always about ignoring the rules. Sometimes it's about following the rules a little *too* closely. Seth Godin provides a perfect example of this in his blog: a customer who's been banking at the same branch for *70 years* has her signature routinely checked whenever she goes in to cash a check.[7]

Are you thoroughly checking new (and old) employees?

Are you keeping an eye on your teams activities?

---

[7] http://sethgodin.typepad.com/seths_blog/2005/08/clueless.html

Ignore the Different Personalities in the Team

Every year at the beginning of the (insert your favorite sport here) season there are all sorts of prognostications about that one team that's destined to win it all. Why will this team be victorious? Because of all the talent it's bought. Yet time and again these dream teams don't live up to their expectations, and often they get defeated by some underdog.

It's the same in the workplace. Throw together a few folks with good reputations and turn them into a dream team—and they'll be sure to succeed. In fact, many of these teams fare no better than those "winning" sports teams.

Successful teams do have talented members—but those members understand each other and draw from each other's strengths. If you're ambitious and you want to see this in action, join a volunteer fire department as active fire fighter. By necessity you'll bond with your team members, and your understanding of teams will change.

Can you describe the personality of each team member?

Do you know what makes them tick?

Do you know how to push their buttons?

I'm Too Busy Right Now...

We've all heard it; and we know it only means we are not a priority right now. While it might be funny in the movies when the hero says he can't deliver the marriage proposal because he's "too busy," it's not funny in business. In fact, it can be a real killer!

Of course there are always situations when the goals of the business and the goals of the team members do not match. Especially lower ranked managers are sitting between the chairs. Neither being an iron man nor hard nose nor everybody's darling leads the business to the desired success. Business and personal goals have to be in harmony.

Who do you please?

And if you please - how do you please?

Are you being used by the team to please them?

Then there is the well known variant:

Laid Back / Let Them Do It...

"Don't come to me with a problem if you don't have the solution!" This is a big bunch of baloney. Not even the most talented staffer will be able to live up to this—at least, not all the time. Besides, a staffer who has all the answers ought to be a manager, right?

Just imagine you sell cars for a living and one of the models you are trying to sell always fails. So you go to your manager to talk about this dilemma. Would your manager expect you to know how to engineer a better model? You might have a few thoughts to share—but a complete overhaul?

Ever heard the claim, "My company doesn't have any problems"? Of course there are problems—even in the best companies! Why doesn't this manager know that there are any? Isn't he in control? A trust company in Germany laid off all its German/English translators; according to their management, "everyone learns English in school." Besides, there were enough bilingual people in the office. A few months later the company had to rehire the translators. What happened? The trust lost the bid for a huge project because of errors in the contract. A typical blunder was the phrase "river diagram" instead of "flow chart diagram." Do you think this is a sign of a management in control?

Are you in control?

Can you gain and keep control?

Do you know some of the problems?

Do you know how to address the problems?

Are you addressing them?

Making Money Is Important.

It's a simple concept: either the company makes money or goes out of business. This is even true for charities and the government! This is very often overlooked because the ways you run a profitable business, a charity, or a country are different. Nonetheless they all have to make sure of the needed funding and encourage the customers/donors/citizens to buy them.

Is making money important for your business?

Are you making money?

Pressing the Budget Too Tight

When you begin with unrealistic budget goals, chaos is bound to set in. Departments fall behind, resources are slow to arrive, and ultimately missions run off the road. The easiest way to avoid having this happen is to create an accurate budget. That means outlining ways to implement better upfront resource planning.

Let me add that it's wrong to meet cost savings with potentially puni-tive measures. What I mean is the old adage "If you don't spend your whole budget this year, you'll get less next year" mindset. If a department has saved money and come in under budget, why not consider giving part of those savings back in the form of bonuses? The upfront cost will be offset by higher productivity, and more cost conscious employees.

Do you have a budget?

Do you review it constantly?

Are employees cost conscious?

Instead of Delegating You Do Everything Yourself

Management by objectives and management by delegation go hand in hand. Is there a need for an employee when the manager does everything? Well, let's think about it in different terms: can any manager dance at 50 weddings at the same time?

At how many weddings are you dancing?

Certainly there will be times when the manager knows best how to do a specific task. But why not take the opportunity to teach the team? Delegation is good management, but it's also a sign of leadership. Often you hear that managers cut their hours significantly once they learned how to delegate effectively. This gives them more time to concentrate on what managers should be thinking about.

Are you taking over tasks from the team or do you teach?

*"Give a man a fish and he will eat for a day. Teach
a man to fish and he will eat for the rest of his life.
Chinese Proverb*

Do you delegate?

Do you consider delegating before you start a task?

Be Everybody's Darling

When a member of the team becomes a manager for the first time, the initial rush gets tempered pretty quickly. The reason? The manager is no longer a "peer" to his or her teammates. Making the transition from peer to leader is more difficult than you might think.

Can there be a distinction between friendship and business? There has to be. The more problematic issue is whether a manager can be a fair boss during the day and a great friend—to the same people—after work. As a peer, the manager could be friends with everyone. As a manager, there have to be boundaries. There are rules that both the manager and the employees have to follow. An employee who tries to exploit a friendship with the manager to get special favors (easier workload, extra time off, a better work space) isn't helping anyone. And if the manager gives in—the message to the rest of the staff is, "It's who you know if you want to get ahead."

Managers have to be respectful of their employees—and vice versa. If an employee gets angry at the manager and becomes verbally abusive, the excuse of "Well, he used to be my friend" won't carry much weight. And if the manager is abusive as well, for the same reason, it sends a bad message to the rest of the staff.

Lead by example if you want to be respected, acknowledged, and appreciated—by everyone you work with.

Do you lead by example?

Do you let friendships take over?

Are all of your employees your best buddies?

Only Give Tribute
to a Chosen Few

How hard can it be for a manager to compliment each employee every once in a while? It costs a business lots more money to replace an employee than to retain one—so why not keep your current employees happy?

Are you keeping them happy?

Now, there will always be some employees who will perform so outstandingly that they just seem to generate more praise than others. There's no question it's important to recognize truly outstanding efforts. But every employee has the potential to go above and beyond in some area. Watch for each employee's strengths and find something to praise.

Watch out for something else as well. Sometimes employees who receive large amounts of praise let it go to their heads. If they take the ongoing tribute as a hint that they're above the law in the company, their merits will quickly fade. So that's another reason not to give the appearance that you're playing favorites.

The manager has to make it very clear that each and every employee plays an important role in the company. *"Both committed and non-committed respondents agreed on the importance to see the organization set examples. For the former, exemplarity was a motivator factor in the sense of Hertzberg (1959) while for the latter the absence of exemplarity was a reason for rejection (as an unsatisfied hygiene factor)".*[8]

The best teachers are those who will always have a good word for everyone; no matter how good or bad the outcome. Can you imagine what would happen if we decided not to encourage the toddler who just starts to walk, no matter how often she falls down in those early attempts?

You are the best horse in my stable...

Who do you motivate?

How do you motivate?

---

[8] Tessa Melkonian, *Change Acceptance: The Role of Exemplarity*, p. 9.
Dr. Melkonian is Associate Professor of Management and Human Resources at the European Institute for LifeLong Learning. She holds a Ph.D. in management from the University of Paris and a degree in clinical psychology from the University of Lyon
.

Minor Sins

Besides the 13 deadly sins there are many others that can cause—at the very least—deep trouble for people trying to work together and run a business. If you combine a few of those, the result might be even worse for your business then having to deal with just one deadly sin.

Respect?

*"Never take a person's dignity: it is worth every-
thing to them, and nothing to you."*
Frank Barron

Many years ago I worked for a man who believed that there were two
kinds of people: himself and the rest of the world. Management was his
"passion" and so was horseback riding. (Come to think of it, I bet he
treated the horses' way better than he treated any human.) You might wonder why I mention his hobby. Many say that horseback riding is a great
example for perfect teamwork. Even to the casual observer it's clear that
the overall performance of a rider and the horse deeply depends on how
good a team they are. Each depends on the other and they both have to pay
attention to each other all the time.

You might think that a horseback rider would be a better manager precisely because riding increases one's understanding of teamwork. That
wasn't the case with this fellow.

The first time I saw him exert his management "style", it was astonish-
ing. He came over to an employee who had made some sort of error. That
wouldn't have been particularly memorable, except that the manager was
armed with a whip—*and he used it!* He actually whipped the worker's
fingers and unleashed a stream of insults at him. (As an aside, this manager eventually became a judge in a court dealing primarily with business

cases.)

What would you do in such a situation?

A manager climbed up the corporate ladder while his former co-worker stayed in the position he was hired for. For a long time, each time this employee came by his office she would just jump in—no matter if the door was closed, a meeting was going on. The manager was too polite (and perhaps too shocked) to say anything, and so the situation persisted. An employee who could invade a manager's private space like that clearly doesn't know the meaning of the word "respect"; or understands true friendship.

> *"A good manager is best when people barely know that he exists. Not so good when people obey and acclaim him. Worse when they despise him."*
> *Lao-Tzu*

Do you respect each and everyone in your team?

More important—does the team think the manager is respecting them?

Do you step in when you see someone being disrespected?

"I'm sorry."

The Associated Press issued an article that hospitals in the University of Michigan Health System have been encouraging doctors since 2002 to apologize for mistakes. The system's annual attorney fees have since dropped from $3 million to $1 million, and malpractice lawsuits and notices of intent to sue have fallen from 262 filed in 2001 to about 130 per year, said Rick Boothman, a former trial attorney who launched the practice there.

Unfortunately this seems to be an isolated incident. The news is full of stories highlighting alls sorts of mistakes made by companies and their employees. Yet what we rarely see is one of the first words children learn (and frequently get told to use):

"Sorry."

When was the last time you said sorry?

When was the last time you as a customer were told "sorry"?

Or one of your team members?

Is sorry part of dealing with disgruntled customers or suppliers?

Listen. Lead. Succeed.

Virtually every great manager I've dealt with during my career is a terrific listener. This is so basic an idea that it's hard to believe there are people who don't place a high value on good listening skills. Who can't point to countless problems—in their own lives and in the lives of others—that developed because someone didn't listen? (For that matter, think of how many problems listening would solve.)

"I like to listen. I have learned a great deal from listening carefully. Most people never listen."
Ernest Hemingway

I'll never forget my first experience with a "listening manager." At first I thought he was just being lazy. His office door was always open and whenever I passed by I could see him sitting at his desk doing—well, doing nothing. This was my first real job, so you can imagine I was pretty surprised and a little disappointed. It wasn't until later that I learned this manager's secret to success: *listening.* He would go around and talk to everyone—really talk. (The first time he came into my office we talked for more than two hours.) By talking to everyone—and by listening—he got a good picture of how things were going, who needed help, who was doing all right, and so on. And he made his decisions based on what he had heard.

Listening seems to be some long lost art, but it doesn't have to be. If you're a parent (or if you know small children), you know that children are happiest with their parents when the parents are taking the time to listen and pay attention to them. Why should it be any different for a business leader?

Is the manager you admire most a great listener?

Do you listen?

Can you listen?

Does the team think the manager is listening? And that management does?

My Title Is My Power: Stepping On Heads

"Education is power," Frederick Douglass said more than a century ago. But by "education" he didn't mean just getting a degree and then coasting on that experience. I know of a chief technology officer who was extraordinarily proud of this Ph.D.—and he wasn't shy about letting people know it. He made the mistake of thinking that he was so educated he didn't need any additional training. Nor, he thought, did his team, since he'd picked each member individually. When a training company approached him, he was dismissive. "I hand-selected every one of my engineers," he said. "They're smart." One of the trainers reminded him that being smart isn't enough if people didn't have the knowledge and training to use their intelligence to its fullest.

The education community often acts as its own worst enemy in this regard. Many countries refuse to accept degrees or certificates awarded in a different country. It's not uncommon for one university to reject the coursework and degrees of another university. At a time when we're being told how education should be more global in scope, how is it global to dismiss the schools of another country? A more forward-thinking approach, I believe, would be if universities embraced more people from other countries or schools. That would give students experience in cultural as well as educational differences.

Personally what counts more for you: knowledge or the title?

And in your company?

Ignorance

The Hardliner

Knows everything, and knows it better than anyone else. Some wonder if the hardliner is nothing more than a fake who's too insecure to confront the reality that he can make mistakes like anyone else. The truth is, most people can spot those who do know and those who only *think* they know.

Do It by the Book

This very often is a product of a strongly regulated environment such as the military. "What you're doing can't be done!" they exclaim, "It's not part of any standard operating procedure!" This sort of manager can have a particularly bad influence in a creative environment.

Predator / Hunter

Dangerous—and dangerous because their real goal at work is to "score"—to get another trophy (much the way a real hunter might). Sometimes predator/hunter types can perform perfectly well. But sometimes the obsession with doing best can paralyze an otherwise intelligent manager.

The Team Freak

This person believes that everything must be a team effort. *Everything.* Don't get me wrong—I think teams are great. But as with anything else, they're great at the appropriate time. Not every activity or decision will be best handled by a team. Sometimes a simple decision can get hopelessly bogged down because the entire team had to examine it at length instead of just one or two knowledgeable people.

The Diplomat

Diplomacy is good, but not when it's used as a thinly veiled way to get out of making decisions. The manager who insists on studying and investigating every project forgets that the competition may be moving faster and gaining speed (and customers).

The Nerd

They may be brilliant and knowledgeable—but often nobody understands what they're talking about! We have all seem them. Everywhere. The problem with nerds is that people don't bother trying to understand them, even when they should be trying to—which is a loss for everyone.

And Then There Are Also:

The Star	Wants to shine but not work.
The Lawyer	What's in it for me?
The Politician	A flip-flopper.
The Cop	Everything needs a rule and rules must be followed.
The Chaos Manager	Only the genius knows how to rule the chaos.
Mr. Clean	Can only work in a sterile office.
The Discriminator	Takes priority based on gender age and even race.

The Opinionated   Their way or the high way.

Step 3

Take Responsibility

What Is Responsibility?

Responsibility: 1. the obligation, readiness, to carry the consequences for an action, either from oneself or another person; 2. the obligation to provide security for someone; 3. the justification for an action; 4. to take someone into account for their action.

How often do we feel that different people have different interpretations of what constitutes responsibility? Does it come from emotional intelligence? Or is it a matter of plain old intuition? To know when and how to take responsibility and make decisions are what really marks someone as a leader. Yet managers know that "responsibility" per se isn't a tangible part of the job description. That's what makes it so hard to define and characterize.

Are you responsible for the market changes?

That things turned out differently?

Does that make you guilty?

> *"Action springs not from thought,*
> *but from a readiness for responsibility."*
> Dietrich Bonhoeffer

Can you define responsibility?

Can your team?

Is it the same?

When and for what are you responsible?

Are you responsible when a co-worker is overwhelmed?

What if that co-worker outranks you in the corporate hierarchy?

Responsibility means being accountable for your own actions—and taking the blame for your mistakes. "Wait a minute," I hear you saying. "Most politicians don't do that." Well, some do, but as for those who don't—well, they're the ones who give politicians a bad reputation.

"Government is like a baby.
An alimentary canal with a big appetite at one end
and no sense of responsibility at the other."
Ronald Reagan

Is a company acting responsibly when it takes on a questionable client in the interest of keeping the business afloat? Or when it accepts a project during a slow period for far less than the usual price just to have some cash flow? Food for thought.

Cool?

"I am responsible for 10 people. Without me..." Doesn't it sound cool to have that sort of responsibility? Well, we all know that the reality is far from cool!

Many managers pay for that level of responsibility with endless meetings, uncounted hours of overtime, and ultimately less time for themselves. Being a manager can be just like being a parent—only that you're a parent to an entire staff. And with employees enjoying more freedom in many ways than they did in the past, sometimes it's hard to get them to do what's expected of them. It's hard for managers to take a break. They're expected to keep things moving—particularly during a downturn in the company. Above all, managers have to do all these things and yet continue to stay clear and focused.

A company with 50 employees got sold to a big player in the market. Management informed the employees of the sale and assured them that nothing would change. More information was promised to come within the next few days.

Days turned into weeks before two executives from the new company came in to address the employees' questions. Trouble is, they *didn't* address their questions. Instead, they talked about themselves and how successful they had been. Questions were ignored.

The old managers were right—things didn't change all that much on a day-to-day basis. But the atmosphere was different. Employees got the impression that the new management just didn't care. It affected morale and productivity, to the extent that within a year most of those employees had found jobs elsewhere.

The new managers missed a great opportunity to engage those employees by making them feel right from the start like part of the company. They went through the motions, but that's never enough. For their ignorance and arrogance, they paid by losing many talented and knowledgeable workers.

Do you care?

Does the team know you do?

Does management come across as ignorant or arrogant?

Responsibility and Its Side Effects

When everything is going well, nobody takes the time to talk about responsibility. That's exactly the time everyone *should* be talking about it. It would help companies map out what they want to do and where they want to be. But when nothing's going wrong, why rock the boat?

At the same time, there are always managers who do understand the importance of being responsible. When they try to carry the weight of that responsibility with little or no help, they end up overwhelmed and overworked. And when people are overwhelmed and overworked, they tend to make some pretty bad judgment calls.

A company paid its employees a bonus based on stock options. All the managers were advised to talk with their team members and explain to them how the bonus was put together and being paid. One manager was just too busy with everything else and didn't want to bother himself with doing it. So his team ended up being told nothing. The result was that when his staffers got their checks with the extra money, they didn't know it was a bonus. Several in fact thought it was an accounting error. When they found out why their paychecks were larger, they were happy, but they were also frustrated.

Let's assume that this manager had 20 people in his team. How long would it have taken to speak to all of them—maybe two or three hours? What he did instead was send the message, "The team isn't important to me." It's hard to maintain a sense of trust and commitment when you're sending that sort of message.

Are your managers managed?

How would you manage this manager?

We'll see.

Shouldn't a manager be able to make decisions? Then what do you make of a manager who answers requests with "We'll see"? That's what you tell a child who wants more candy. But what it says to an employee is, "Your question isn't important enough for me to give you an answer." That's a message that can only crush morale and trust. A manager who thinks a brush-off like "We'll see" has bypassed a potential problem has actually created another one by being so cavalier.

"You can delegate authority,
but not responsibility."
Stephen W. Comiskey

How often do you see staff being brushed off?

Working Too Hard

Is it the responsibility of the manager or the team members to take action and try to modify the behavior of workaholics in the group? The workaholic neglects family and other relationships to devote all his or her time to the job. From a productivity standpoint that may not seem to be a bad thing. But consider that if the workaholic can neglect one part of his or her life to fixate on another, how long before he or she fixates on something else and neglects the job at hand? If the workaholic is actually disrupting the workplace, then it's the manager's duty to create clear boundaries.

"If you want children to keep their feet on the
ground, put some responsibility on their shoulders."
Abigail Van Buren

Too often, managers think that letting go is the same as losing control. We all know overprotective parents can't let go, even though letting go is what would be best for their children. And we all know how some of those children turn out: hardly able to make a decision on their own. How much better for those children if they had been allowed to fail sometimes and learn life's lessons on their own. It's the same in the workplace. If the manager never gives the employees any responsibility, trust, and challenges, the employees will be paralyzed.

Learning to be responsible is a lengthy and often difficult process for children. For adults who aren't given the chance to be responsible, it's frustrating to have someone else make all the decisions for them. Managers need to give employees the chance to succeed—and to fail. When the employees make mistakes (and they will), the smart manager will see it as an opportunity to learn. Don't play the blame game with your employees. Ask them *"What happened?"* Find the answers. You can become an interrogator—of the gentle sort. Remember how adept Lt. Columbo was at finding things out, by being non-threatening almost to a fault: "Just one more thing…"

Finding the *right* answers at the right time is all what responsibility is about.

Whose Responsibility Is It Anyway?

Security and privacy have become huge issues in the last decade-especially as they affect electronic storage of personal data. Allow me to tell you a story about a software company that provided packages to government agencies. Access was limited to those who had a user ID and password, and there were other standard high-security safeguards in place. Sounds fine, right?

Well, one of the senior programmers discovered a glitch in the package—a glitch that could seriously compromise the security. Basically, non-registered users could bypass the login system. They would be able to access sensitive personal data quite easily.

You would think that this programmer's discovery would have been taken seriously, right? Think again. He went to his direct supervisor and also to the person in charge of testing the software. What do you think he was told? "It's not your job to search the system for bugs."

He decided to fix the bug himself, on his own time. But he reasoned that if there was one bug, there might be more. He voiced his concerns and his quite reasonable warning to his colleagues. Here are the answers he got:

Lead programmer A: *Not my responsibility.*
Lead programmer B: *I am not getting paid to do that.*
Director of development: *I don't care. Put it in when it works...*

Chief Technology Officer: *As long as the customer does not find out about it we really don't have to fix it. Stop wasting time on finding bugs!*

Excuse me?

Wouldn't you think that management would be pleased and relieved that the problem was found—and solved—internally, before it became public?

Here's a situation where nobody (except for that lone programmer) was willing to take even the most basic responsibility. If there's a problem with the product, it should be the responsibility of *everyone* to watch for it, to report it, and (if possible) to correct it. That doesn't mean employees have to spend all their time looking for bugs. A few simple safeguards can minimize the problem:

1. Increase the amount of product testing.
2. Train employees on ethical behavior.
3. Improve the lines of communication within and between teams.
4. Make the customers' needs the top priority.
5. Be honest about mistakes and fix them as soon as possible.
6. Encourage employees to take initiative.

Do you take responsibility?

Do your employees?

One of the Ritz-Carlton Basics states that a complaint has to be handled by the employee who received that complaint. That gives the employee immediate responsibility. It's also a valuable step at a time when so many customers see the employee they deal with as "the company." As responsibility increases, employees identify themselves more with the business—which means they'll have more of an incentive to do their best.

Blame Is Not an Option

A lot of effort is spent in playing games instead of getting the work done. Probably the most dangerous is the blame game. No other game leaves employees feeling more demoralized and unproductive—both of which lead to poor performance.

> *"When you can't solve the problem, manage it."*
> *Robert Schuller*

You offer solutions, and no one listens. Yet as soon as things aren't working out, you get blamed. If you ask questions, you may still be told it's your fault. Sound familiar? Sadly, it happens all the time.

Do you have room for answers?

Isn't it funny that no matter what causes a problem, all the excuses are the same?
1. It wasn't me.
2. It was her / him.
3. They get paid too much.
4. I'm not getting paid enough.
5. They don't work hard enough.

6.   They have me doing too much.

7.   (No doubt you can add several of your own...)

Now, what about finding out what's going wrong while the project is still active? Well, some people will play around with various models to find out what could have happened if they had changed parameters. A great idea when you're studying a model—but when you're dealing with a real problem, right now, you don't have time to spend trying to recast the entire project. One question teams don't like to ask is, "If all the parameters we're working with are bad, how come all the other teams are doing fine working with the exact same parameters?" For some teams, that question is too dangerous to ask.

More often than we'd like to hear, management blames the human costs (in other words, the size of the workforce). Very often that always leads to the painful and frequently wrong decision to lay off workers. The rationale is always that the remaining employees will just have to work harder. (Not that they have any incentive to want to at that point, except to keep their jobs.) Getting the biggest win doesn't necessarily happen with the smallest amount of resources.

Interestingly, a recent study found that by *paying its employees more*, Costco gets lower turnover and higher productivity. That, coupled with a business strategy that includes a mix of higher-margin products, enables Costco to keep its labor costs lower than Wal-Mart's as a percentage of sales.

The blame game is often met with an equally problematic game: "Let's put this off." Problems that get carried from one project to the next, from one meeting to the next, never get solved. *Never*. Eventually, the pervading message becomes "Those who work make mistakes; those who do not work make no mistakes." If you're the manager in a situation like this, you actually *should* take most of the blame. A strong manager who's willing to get past the games and drive the team will get the most out of that team.

> *"A chief is a man who assumes responsibility.*
> *He says 'I was beaten,'*
> *he does not say 'My men were beaten' "*
> *Antoine de Saint-Exupéry*

Remember that part of responsibility is getting others to take their share. Managers can offer solutions, but they should encourage the team to come up with solutions as well. Don't allow the team to get caught up in the blame game. Work together to solve the problems that come up, and make it clear to the team that each member bears responsibility for the project and whether it succeeds.

What to Do When the Boss Is a Failure

What indeed. Well, you can always run away. Get a new job—maybe even one with more money and better benefits. Of course, you have no guarantee that in your new job the boss will not be an even bigger failure. But more importantly, consider what running away will do to your reputation—among your colleagues and among your team members. Making a move under these circumstances might actually slow down your career.

Just as your success is tied to your team, your boss's success is tied to you.

What makes a good manager? Creativity, competence, knowledge, and charisma are just a few of the many characteristics we hear in response to this question. Managers who perform badly are missing at least some of those. They procrastinate and tend to keep themselves away from everything that might be threatening to their position. At least in their minds. Let us not forget that procrastinating can be an extremely powerful tactic. Mostly used by politicians and often seen in sports like cycling.

Do you avoid making decisions?

Where do you stand in the company?

Highly skilled specialists are often put into management positions in the mistaken belief that their expertise will make up for their lack of managerial experience. Unfortunately, few of them can make the transition to manager without the right training—no matter how talented they may be in other areas. Consider the case of one small company that appointed three professionals, all lacking managerial experience, to management positions. Top management promised management training. Unfortunately, that "training" amounted to two days of formal training in two years. It was frustrating to the "managers," who were aware of their shortcomings and who genuinely wanted to be trained. And it was frustrating to their employees because things suffered under well-intentioned but ineffective leadership.

What was top management's reason for being so stingy with training? They felt that training was too costly and that most managers learn on the job anyway. A poor excuse for a poor decision.

When was your last management training?

Does it help to go over someone's head to complain? It depends on the organization. Organizations with a rigid structure (think of the military) discourage or may not allow it, instead offering some representative to answer questions and sort out complaints. And of course, if the company doesn't really care about complaints, it may never even reach a truly listening ear.

Are complaints dropped?

Are you trained to deal with complaints?

A small business owner needed a greater credit line from his bank. Instead of continuing to deal with his reluctant advisor at the bank he went to the branch manager and closed the deal. But at the end of the meeting the branch manager said: "I need to run this by your advisor." Naturally the advisor didn't decline, but he still complained later to the small business owner that he went directly to the branch manager.

Who do you think lost face?

Set priorities! Sounds easy—but how often is it really done? And even when priorities are set, are they acted upon? More important, are those priorities in harmony with the company's goals? With your own goals? It's often hard to set aside the time to get everything done that you need to do, but unless you set priorities and stick to them, you'll never have time to complete any of them.

Do you have the right priorities?

Does your boss?

Instead of being frustrated with the boss, how can you help create a more productive environment? One way is with praise. *Praise?* That's right. I don't mean undeserved praise. What I mean is this: suppose you're not pleased with some new procedure the boss has implemented. You could confront the boss and say how you feel. How far do you think that would get you? Bosses don't like being criticized. But if you present your complaint in a nicer package, you may have better luck. Start with a compliment. Don't be insincere or smarmy, just point out something that you think the boss deserves an extra "thanks" for. *Then* you can mention your complaint—except that you should phrase it as a suggestion. The boss may not agree to your idea, but you haven't been arrogant or disrespectful, so you'll likely be taken more seriously.

When was the last time you complimented your boss?

Smiled?

If you want to minimize the risk that your team starts viewing you as a failure, remember these keys to being a good manager:

1. Be flexible
2. Be creative
3. Be open
4. Look to help without your advantage in mind
5. Be a partner instead of an enemy
6. Listen and *hear*
7. Learn

"When the boss is away, work becomes a holiday".
Portuguese Proverb

Step 4

What Do You Pay

Respect

One of the most important factors for an enjoyable working environment is respect. Employees—and employers—have a right to be treated fairly, equally, and with dignity. And no team can function properly if the members don't respect one another.

There should be no tolerance—none—for harassment, discrimination, or any kind of behavior that compromises anyone's dignity in the workplace. Nor should this kind of behavior be allowed to exist between the employees and the company's vendors and suppliers. It is one of the manager's primary duties to stop this sort of behavior as soon as it crops up, and to ensure an atmosphere of sensitivity and respect. Remember the manager I talked about earlier who liked to whip his employees? Behavior like that, from any source, is completely unacceptable.

> *"If you have some respect for people as they are,*
> *you can be more effective in helping them to be-*
> *come better than they are."*
> *John W. Gardner*

A manager lacking people skills probably shouldn't be a manager. Too often managers are selected solely based on their education or business skills like planning, organizing, and strategic thinking. Those are all crucial skills—but how can a manager get anything accomplished without being able to reach out to people effectively? (And remember that means reaching out to customers and clients, too.) Efficient leadership isn't learned and executed from a few specific lessons. It takes people skills to gain the trust and the loyalty of the employees and the customers.

Are you loyal?

Are the members of the team?

Your customers?

Do you reach out?

Overtime is a fact of life in many companies, and in truth there are many employees who work overtime willingly (even when it's unpaid time) because they want to make sure the project they're working on gets done right. You would think that this would delight managers. Instead, many times managers insist on exerting control over these overtime hours. You can imagine that the employees don't feel too motivated after that.

When is overtime really overtime?

Let us assume you have a project estimated with 40 hours to complete.

Do you expect a senior person to finish within 20 hours?

A junior person within 60 hours?

Are those twenty additional hours from the junior overtime?

What do you want the senior person to do when finishing early?

Are you calculating hours based on the seniority of the worker?

Does presence at work count as working time?

Have you ever put your personality and your private life completely on hold while you're at work? Probably not. Personality plays a big role in how we do our jobs. And for some people, part of their personality might include talking—a lot. One manufacturing company had two employees who seemed to be spending most of their time just chatting with each other. Well, they were—and not always about business-related issues. But partly because of the rapport they developed, and partly because of the information they shared, they managed to be among the best troubleshooters in the company. Top management didn't see it that way and instructed them to keep their chatting to a minimum. They did as they were instructed to do—and their productivity levels plummeted. Do you think their managers ever understood how badly they actually hurt the business?

Now, there's a fine line here between people who talk with each other to keep their minds actively engaged in what they're doing and people who just like to gossip. Managers do have a right to know which it is. The amount and quality of the work produced should serve as a good clue.

Great managers show interest in employees by:

1. Being very clear in what they expect and what they do not accept.
2. Being open—even when the topic is difficult.
3. Taking the time to sit down with their people and evaluate their work.
4. Listening and *hearing*.
5. Helping find solutions.
6. Encouraging feedback.
7. Accepting constructive criticism.

Sometimes employees can be their own worst enemies. The fast-food employee who says, "I'm just a burger flipper" should remember that if those burgers don't get flipped, customers will go to a place that doesn't sell half-burned burgers. It's up to management to recognize when employees are feeling as though their role isn't that important. Managers should remind employees that *every* job has value and if even the smallest task isn't taken seriously it will have an impact on the project's overall success.

Protection

Do you protect the members of your team? What I mean is, do you give them the peace of mind to be able to do their jobs at their best? Sometimes that may mean giving them leeway that top management won't readily understand—but the manager has to make the judgment call. One manager in a *Fortune* 50 company allowed an employee to spend countless hours chatting with others or playing computer games. Yet he allowed this to go on. Why did he let this employee do things *his* way? Because the employee was his best engineer. "He once disappeared for two hours and then came back and fixed a problem in four hours that would have "taken a week to fix," explained the manager. "Of course I let him do it his way!"

Of course, managers need to make it clear to the others that this doesn't give them the right to be egocentric. So a little bit of discipline might drive home to the employee that he shouldn't expect special treatment whenever he wants it.

Money, Money, Money...

How is this for a bonus: a company had all its employees work overtime for several weeks, including weekends and during holidays. The project was completed in record time (later it was revealed that top management lied about the deadline to give people more incentive to put in all those overtime hours)—and those hard-working staffers got a well-earned bonus of—are you ready?—four hours off.

What kind of bonus have you received / given?

> *"This job is only a test,*
> *had it been an actual job, you would have received*
> *raises, bonuses and promotions."*
> *Anonymous*

Raises

How much pay is too much? Many employees have no idea how much they are worth to the company they work for. They have a pretty good idea of how much they can ask for in the market. But how realistic is that value? Some say that big companies pay more in benefits and cash. But how does that compare with the relative flexibility most small companies offer?

Often company policy dictates that raises be given out only once a year—typically at the end or the beginning of the fiscal year. Employers will often defend the size of the salaries they pay by claiming that the salaries must be fair or else the employees will leave. While this might be true for professions with regulated income (government jobs, for example), this is an illusion in the free job market. People will accept an income they might otherwise reject as inappropriate for a great many reasons. Just because they accept and stay does not mean they consider the pay rate fair.

Are you paying / being paid based on actual skills?

Some employees will try to get job offers to prove to their managers that they are underpaid and can do better elsewhere. Some are strong negotiators—they'll ask for a raise and get it. And some will just wait for the raise to happen, whatever its value. This results in a rather incoherent pay mix:

1. The well paid who are able to get offers from other companies
2. The strong negotiator whose income is based more on their negotiating skills than their working skills. (You do understand that *those people are in the wrong position* at that company, right?)
3. The worker bees who do not open their mouths because they're too busy working

It's to avoid these inconsistencies that many companies simply give raises only once a year. This may buy some time, but it doesn't solve the problem. Ultimately, some employees will lose their motivation, and others will simply leave.

When raises are given only once a year, often so are evaluations. (Major milestones, such as anniversaries or the completion of an important project, aren't figured in to the date.) Because people forget what happened through the entire year, this sort of evaluation procedure is as unfair as the scoring of the last few seconds of a round in boxing: the most recent happenings are remembered best.

Evaluations should be done *continuously*. After all this is the best way for the manager to control what the employees do and help them to grow. Remember—the better the employee does, the better the manager looks.

What options does a manager have? Company policies might not allow managers to give a raise outside the norm. Evaluations on the other hand can be done always—no one is keeping managers from doing them.

Do you know what really motivates your people?

Does that qualify for a bonus?

Are all treated equally when it comes to bonuses?

Are you paying a bonus after every finished project / reached milestone?

Do you evaluate during and after a project?

Are your bonuses always monetary?

Step 5

Make Your Team Work

Teams

Manchester Inc., a consulting firm near Philadelphia, surveyed more then 825 human resource managers nationwide to find that 82% of the respondents named *the failure to build partnerships and teamwork* the number one problem confronting newly appointed managers.

Successful teams need more then just one leader. Despite the fact that the team as a unit is responsible for teamwork, there will always be tasks that have to be completed by a subgroup of the team. The timely and successful completion of those tasks is necessary for the survival of a winning team. One could even call those subgroups "mini-teams."

> *"Obstacles are those frightful things you see when
> you take your eyes off your goal."*
> *Henry Ford*

A crucial element of teamwork is that the team members have to understand and be willing to take responsibility. And they have to be open to constructive criticism. There are actually a handful of reasons why team members resist taking responsibility. Failure to address those issues will lead to problems within the team, and eventually the team will become dysfunctional. Before taking any steps to fix the team, make sure you understand the real issues.

Do the team members understand their responsibilities?

Do you know why they do not want to take responsibility?

Do they agree with their tasks?

Is there trust?

Creating a successful team and keep it a success is hard work for the whole team. You can't just throw a group of people together and call them a team. Certain minimum conditions must be fulfilled:
1. True communication
2. Engagement of each team member for and in the team
3. The will to learn and explore
4. Structure
5. Coordination

Even when you have all those elements, you still don't have a team yet. The members have to bond together tightly. Although that bond only focuses on specific goals, when working on those goals the team members need to work together with much of the same intensity and commitment you'd find in a marriage. To better bond the team, some teams will even consider the help of psychologists (an option TV viewers saw in 2004 on NBC's show "The Restaurant") to overcome obstacles.

It costs time—and money—to design an effective team. The biggest obstacle to effective teams is impatience. Often, team members think that everything should be perfect, right from the beginning. Going back to the marriage analogy for a moment, how many people get married after the first date? And remember also that even the best marriages can run into problems—problems that both parties need to work together to solve. It's the same with teams, except that there are more people involved. Even though the team members are united in a common goal, that doesn't minimize the complexity of the group—or the work involved in getting everyone to cooperate. The best teams are those whose members understand that it take constant work and effort to achieve their goals.

Do you work on your team—daily?

The Shotgun Team

Designing a team means to find the right person for the right job. In business we can find plenty of examples of how teams under-perform—and many of those under-performing teams are in trouble simply because nobody ever bothered to design the team and fit the members. In general the most successful teams are those where the leader has the ability to replace members that are not a fit. Remember that the team has to work together as one. You can get angry with a friend or loved one and not speak for a couple of weeks and then make up and move on. You don't have that luxury of time with a team. If communication is allowed to break down, the team will become dysfunctional.

How often have you been in a team that was dysfunctional?

And how often in a functional one?

How well do you think a "shotgun team" works? About as well as a shotgun wedding! Out of need, a few people are thrown together and named a "team." Then the manager (parent) walks away and expects things to work out. Odds are they won't. Of course, a manager who would walk away from a shotgun team is probably not above letting the team take the blame when things go wrong. After landing a multi-million dollar project, the managers in one firm did not follow their lead team designer's carefully crafted advice. They had him spend almost a week creating a plan that included a detailed timetable and budget, as well as guidelines for designing the right team. For whatever reason, management decided to delegate running the team to less experienced employees, one of whom was named team leader. Because no one had the needed experience in running a team, it faltered, and even though a manager was finally brought in to lead the team, by then costs had risen and deadlines had been missed.

The project was way over budget, finished almost a year late and the result was—well, the company is no longer in business anymore. (By the way, the original plan was cheaper, used fewer resources, and had a more reasonable time frame.)

Of course there will always be examples of dysfunctional teams that actually tackle a project and pull it off. But at what price? Burning out employees to get a project done is in no one's interest. For starters, how will those employees perform on their next project? At the end of the 1980s there was a famous "business model" for software companies: sell a software package and once enough sales are in—you program that software. Great—all of your development is paid for and you never lose any money. Of course, there was one small problem: the deadline stress and the amount of overtime were so ridiculously high that employee turnover at these companies was enormous. Many programmers would quit after finishing just one project.

Are your team members a fit for the team?

Was every team member interviewed for a specific job in that team?

Are you willing to vote members out because they don't fit?

Can you?

How much time was spent designing the team?

Team Performance

One factor often used to validate the success or functionality of a team is the team performance. You measure either with passive criteria (subjective valuations of team members) or active criteria (results, quality, etc.). Of course, one element of performance is what the team's specific task happens to be at any given time. Teams may provide a variety of tasks, and the team leader should let the members know precisely what measurements will be used to evaluate performance—and whether those measurements will change with each project.

The success of any team depends on a lot of dynamics. Christoph Haug, an organizational development expert based in Germany, has identified two primary dynamics in teams, which he calls *soft factors* and *hard factors*. Hard factors can be more tangibly measured than soft factors—yet soft factors often appear to be more important to the team.

Do you know the soft and hard factors?

Soft Factors

There are quite a few of what we call soft factors. Let's focus here on the most important ones: vision, communication, support, and emotion.

Vision

> *"The very essence of leadership is*
> *that you have to have a vision."*
> Theodore Hesburgh

A team without a vision is a waste of time. The vision maps out the how, when, and—for some most important—why. The manager's job is not only to communicate the vision to the team, but to get each member to accept the vision as his or her vision as well.

The vision is what gets the team personally involved. Once the team members understand the vision and see it as their vision, there will be stronger involvement, dedication, and motivation. And— things will quickly fall into place, as soon as the team starts to see the vision as its vision and not just the manager's vision.

Does everyone know the vision?

Do they have to know the vision?

Communication

*"The art of communication
is the language of leadership."*
James Humes

It's no exaggeration to say that too often in companies the left hand really doesn't know what the right hand is doing. The problem: poor communication. When communication is done poorly (or not at all) the result is a project that has no plan. When there's no plan, deadlines are missed, budgets are overextended, customers are unhappy, employees are angry and exhausted, and managers have to clean up the mess. Remember that communication doesn't have to be positive. Some managers (and team members) think that only good news should be communicated. *Wrong.* The important thing about communication is that it has to be open and honest. Communicating a problem is the only way to let people know there's a problem that has to be solved.

Does your team suffer from dishonesty?

Or lack of communication?

In some industries it's not uncommon for engineers to promise a delivery date that they know is unrealistic. Ultimately, the delivery is late; the customers are angry and the engineers who promised the missed date look bad.

If managers are pushing people to make unrealistic promises like this, they'll develop a reputation as bullies who have to threaten or scare their employees into working.

Are you seen as a bully?

Can you explain the dynamics of your business?

When communication is poor there are no winners. To avoid communication breakdowns, it has to contain elements of positive (not personal) criticism, partnership instead of self-centeredness, and most important the support of the entire team. Sadly enough, many managers think that forcing team members to participate is the solution. Just think back to all the moments you've seen people do this—in school, in relationships, in sports, and in politics.

Can you remember any of those efforts succeeding?

Forcing people to participate doesn't take into consideration the different personalities of team members. What people say—and don't say—is often a reflection of how they conduct themselves professionally. There are plenty of quiet people who may say only one thing during a meeting—but that one point becomes the most important one brought up. A midsize team at a *Fortune* 100 company had a Monday morning meeting to verify the progress of its latest project. The team leader constantly picked on one member for being lazy and not being finished with his task. That member actually was finished, having spent all weekend on the task at hand. But the leader refused to let him speak. No other member said a word. Clearly they figured, "Why bother?" Ultimately what could have been a productive meeting turned into the leader's monologue, and nothing got accomplished.

Is criticism in your team constructive or personal?

How fast is information spread? Faster or slower than rumors?

Are all team members willing to communicate openly?

Is every team member knowledgeable about his or her own strengths and weaknesses?

Do team members stand up for each other?

Support

Can a business afford to employ people just for the sake of employing them? You would think not—but consider what the leader of a *Fortune 50* company once said about his employees; they could be busy for two years, he believed, without ever taking care of even one customer and not really knowing their role in what the company does.

Do companies really support the talents they employ?

Or is it more like the hunter who is satisfied the moment another trophy is added to the collection?

> *"My first thoughts are that I should not let people down, that I should support them and love them."*
> *Diana, Princess of Wales*

An engineer had to give up his office to a manager. He was put into a space with other engineers, and he missed his privacy. But what he missed more was the whiteboard he used to make his notes and calculations. The manager didn't need the whiteboard, but she decided that since it had come with the office she was going to keep it anyway. The engineer wasn't all that surprised. After all, the way he found out he was losing his office was in a brief e-mail sent the day of the move.

Do you think that engineer was still delivering at his best?

Remember the sins?

The engineer's manager felt no responsibility to him, nor did he take into account how demoralized the engineer would feel losing his office.

Sometimes companies try to deny their staffers even the most basic tools—trade magazines and books (and bookcases to put them on) for example. In the software industry, developers often have a hard time getting licenses and other critical equipment.

Is all of your software licensed?

Is all your equipment officially allowed?

A company got a 17-inch monitor for one of its developers—making her the only developer who didn't have a 15-inch screen. Many software developers will tell you that the administrative staff has better and newer equipment than they do.

Another company found out that it was spending $2,000 a year on coffee for its employees. The free coffee ended, but the company allowed each employee ten minutes a day to go get coffee from someplace else. The loss in productivity that resulted probably cost the company a lot more than the cost of that coffee.

Not that all employees are saints. Some can be quite wasteful with the company's resources. Paper and pens disappear regularly. Companies' phone bills can be exorbitant. Some companies do ask their employees to pay for personal calls. But even if they do, the time spent making those calls adds up pretty quickly. And of course, there are the employees who call "900" numbers or who use the Internet to surf adult content and gambling sites. Wouldn't it be fair to say these employees do not take responsibility seriously?

Are the team members using the resources thoughtfully?

Does the team have enough resources?

Does the team have the right tools?

Emotions

"Flowers are restful to look at.
They have neither emotions nor conflicts."
Sigmund Freud

To avoid the power games every team faces the team members have to be open emotionally and (to the extent they can be) unbiased. Individuals tend to hide behind a façade because they fear criticism or humiliation. That's why openness is so important.

An open team:

1. Handles problems quickly and solves them without time-consuming small talk.
2. Considers openness an important element of the team's strength.
3. Empowers every member to grow.
4. Works faster.
5. Criticizes constructively.
6. Is goal-oriented.
7. Is fun (yes, fun) for all involved.

The main role of the leader in an open team is to ensure that the openness does not turn into a "let me tell you how bad..." war between the members. It is about the ability to criticize without needing to destroy.

Hard Factors

Hard factors are the objective and empirical measurable factors.

Goals

Unfortunately team members are often overlooked during the goal setting process. This is a mistake. The more you can unite the team members and their personal goals into the goal of the team, the more likely you can succeed in the long run. Let's take a look at unrealistic and undesirable goals:

1. Goals that are defined after the work is done
2. Continuously changing members
3. Continuously changing goals to match the work of the team
4. Nebulous intentions
5. Wishful thinking
6. Fuzzy ideas
7. Alibi-goals

If your goals are neither precise nor measurable, you're setting yourself up for a disaster. Imprecise goals leave room for different interpretations and misunderstandings. If you can't measure you can neither control nor check the team's progress. On top of that, you will not be able to divide the team for subtasks—after all, you don't know the main task.

Are the right goals defined?

Do you provide your team with the right goals?

Team Leadership

Teamwork is not necessarily a democratic activity. Yes, often the teams vote on who will lead, but the leader's role is to make decisions and keep the team working instead of debating. It should be the manager's top priority to find a team leader who has the necessary competencies. Too often teams are dysfunctional just because the leader is given no authority to rule against a problem team member: "You're not my boss—you can't tell me anything!" Once the other team members see this, the damage has been done. Bringing in another leader can work, but it rarely does. Usually you have to break up and re-form the team.

How many teams have you seen with leaders who have little or no authority?

Rotating Leaders

Some teams work not only very well but actually better with rotating team leaders. It usually works best when the members have worked together for a while and are familiar with each other's strengths and weaknesses. The static leadership will be replaced with a more flexible one. The team members will be acting more independently, but also perhaps more respectfully. Some see the different competencies of the rotating leaders as the biggest strength.

The static leadership role is always bound to a single person. If that person fails or falls out of favor, the team will be headless and at best perform well below its expectations. With rotating leadership at least there is always a viable and knowledgeable replacement available.

Would you consider rotating leaders?

Planning

Time, budget and resource planning are the foundation every team needs to perform. Especially non-rotating leadership teams suffer from the unwillingness to share any of the planning with the members. Out-of-the-loop employees are less disciplined and cause planning stress, in part because they never had a chance to include the team planning into their personal planning.

Deadlines in the software industry are the perfect example of poor planning: someone decides what a "reasonable" time-frame should be and then the team has to work toward it. And you don't have to be in the software industry to know how often desired deadlines get missed.

Many entrepreneurs think that they are not part of a team because they work alone. But what about their accountants, suppliers and customers? Their life partners and friends? It may not be exactly the same, but these are "teams" as well. So everyone has at least some experience with how teams work.

Many managers think that they are not part of a team—they truly feel that it is lonely at the top. They would do better to view the "top" as a resting plateau that comes before the next upward climb. And no doubt they had help from others during their career track (think team again).

Are you planning with or without the team?

Step 6

Change, Growth and Trust

Change

A while ago I spoke at a Rotary Club meeting. A longtime member took part in the discussion for (I later found out) the first time ever. He felt safe enough to participate and was delighted that he could share a story. It was fascinating to see the dropping jaws of all the other members when he spoke up.

How often do you make your silent team members speak up?

Do they feel comfortable with you?

Do they feel safe?

Do they trust you?

Can the group keep secrets?

What do the answers above tell you about your group?

Encouraging employees is important, and it can also be exhilarating. It's all about people, their dreams, their potential and their strong sides. Do not force them into being something they're not. Create a "playground" where they can practice their strong sides, learn, and understand their value and blossom.

One manager told me: *"Recently I had this experience where I was about to "force" a person into a role he refused to play in a "playground" he could not be in. Happily I caught the signal and made a new playground for him. Now he's on fire and he even got another person involved, who is also on fire. They're creative, bubbling and totally optimistic about the future, without my interference. It's so fun to watch."*

> *"We have been taught to believe that negative equals realistic and positive equals unrealistic."*
> *Susan Jeffers*

A similar effect can be seen during the majority of brainstorming sessions: most people soon start to value ideas as good, bad, mediocre etc. But that only kills the brainstorming. What you really want is to collect every idea and seriously consider every single one of them.

Breaking the rules, and sometimes making your own rules, will help you get off the treadmill of everyday ideas. When it is harder to follow a rule then not to follow it, I take that as a good sign the rule needs to be changed.

Where is breaking the rules seen as bad?

In the upper management or in the mid/lower management?

Keep in mind that *trust* and *rules* are two different things. A great many managers think they must trust their advisors. But what they really need is to be able to question the advice they get so that they can learn from it and make the best decisions that they can.

If you're the one giving advice and you advise to stay within all the rules, what makes your advice different from everyone else's? By offering some alternatives, you're showing that you actually *thought* about the issue at hand.

Are you more effective by upsetting people?

Or by making things easier for those who like to get upset?

Is it important that they might get upset?

What you need sometimes is a manager who's willing to take the big risk and just implement it.

Are you taking risks?

Out of fear most managers don't.

Adding Extra Focus

In his book *Think and Grow Rich* (Aventine Press, 2004), Napoleon Hill introduces readers to the concept of "mastermind groups." While Hill's interpretation is innovative, the actual concept of such a group has been around a long time. Let me share some of the basics here. Basically you get together a group of highly committed people working toward a specific goal. (Not unlike a team.)

The best working mastermind group will consist of five people. At every meeting (these should be held weekly), everyone gets a timeslot to open up and present a problem for the others to solve. The meetings can be fantastic and the results can be quite valuable. Unfortunately most of these groups don't stay together long-term, but while they are together they can get plenty accomplished.

Have you ever created a group like this at work?

Transformed a team by giving it this level of commitment to one problem?

Most managers are rather afraid of change because the time you are most vulnerable to a rival's attack is during times of internal changes. Don't let that fear get the better of you. Instead, turn it around and change faster and better then the competition can. Then it won't matter if your rivals go after you.

Get yourself and your staffers out of the comfort zones. That's how you'll learn and grow.

Are you ready to change and grow?

When was your last change?

Space Clearing

Have you ever thought about how much time you spend with your family and how much time you spend in the office? Most people spend at least half their waking hours during the week at the office. Yet the majority of the workplaces are pretty sterile and devoid of personality. Many employers simply don't allow anyone to bring in personal items (except perhaps a photo or two). You have no opportunity to display who you are—your personality. Imagine if your house were as sterile as your office. As I'll discuss later, different personality types have different approaches to how they maintain their work space. The important thing to remember is that your space has to work for you. Otherwise, you won't truly be comfortable—and considering how much time most of us spend in the office, that's too much time to be uncomfortable.

How Empty Is Your Desk?

Probably the worst management "style" I know comes from a top European manager whose philosophy was that a good worker is recognizable by the emptiness of his or her desk. Every day the manager would walk through his offices to make sure the desks were empty. Whenever he saw a desk with anything more than the essentials-keyboard, monitor, mouse, phone—he would just wipe everything off the desk with a grand gesture—swoosh! All the papers sorted neatly during the day landed on one big pile. Any employee who had the misfortune of having a day's worth of neatly stacked papers ready to file would end up having to put all those pages back in order. You can imagine how (1) the demand for desk drawers increased immensely, and (2) five minutes before the day was over people would frantically put all their paperwork into those drawers. Increased productivity? I don't think so!

My own desk has its empty spots—and its not so empty spots.

How empty is your desk?

> *"Happiness is a very small desk*
> *and a very big wastebasket".*
> *Robert Orben*

Do you think that a totally empty desk really does the job? Some say having an empty desk proves that you run your life without burden. That it makes life easier. But isn't it true that it's just a different life from that of a person with a messy desk? Actually, if you think about it, some of the most cluttered offices are those of the leaders. Desks and bookcases are overflowing, and often the floor gets used for more space.

So how true is it that the human designs the environment and the environment designs the human? Apparently very true! Remember of course that different people have different needs and tasks. Some need the chaos to be more creative, while others find that being organized makes them more effective. Neither way seems to have a real advantage over the other. One thing is certain: when people are forced to organize (or disorganize), it never really works. The messy worker who's told to clean things up, or the organized worker who's told to lighten up, are being asked to exist in an environment that doesn't suit them. Not an efficient use of time. Usually it only takes a few days before everything is back where it was before.

Do you force your style onto others?

Adding storage to store what you don't need in the first place is a waste of resources. Understand the way you work and make the best of it. If you haven't used something for years, how high are the chances you'll need it tomorrow? Do you keep things that are broken or that simply don't work? Why? That birthday card you got from your co-workers 20 years ago—it was a nice gesture but perhaps you can take it home if you really need to save it.

Remember—you are responsible for the clutter around you. Your mom is not coming anymore and cleaning up after you, and neither will your spouse. Some of the clutter will keep your mind busy. With—shall we say needless—things? The same way you can de-clutter your desk, your home, your car, you can also de-clutter your mind and your business.

You can recognize a few of peoples' personality clues from their working space:

1. *The Nomad*

    Nomads can't survive without laptop and other portable tools. Clutter immediately disappears in the virtual trash bin. They tend to be superficial.

2. *The Structurer*

    Structurers are very conscientious. Their desks are usually empty. Books in the bookcases, files are lined up like Marine recruits. You rarely see something personal. The message is clear: work is duty but not joy.

3. *The Creative Genius*

    Clutter is all over the place. Interestingly enough, a great many creative geniuses know exactly what to find in which pile.

4. *The Relaxer*

    You step in their office and wonder, "Does this person live here?" There will be plants, coffee mugs, bric-a-brac, and plenty of pictures (drawings, too, if there's a small child at home).

Of course a person's background and their personal relationships play an important role in recognizing the types. Yes, types, because everyone has a dominant type and at least one other type. Tidiness is always deeply bound to a personality. Do not force your team to go with your kind of rules regarding what is clutter and what not. Instead help the team to live by a few questions:

Is this item really needed?

Does this item help you in your life?

Is this item still state-of-the-art?

Why do you need this item at all?

Do you need this item to feel good?

Do you see the same pattern in a team member's thinking?

Territory

So, what will happen when you put a Nomad and a Creative Genius together in one room? What about on the same team? How about two Creative Geniuses in one room or even in cubicles? It's obvious that a lot of friction between employees can easily avoided by familiarizing them with the different personality types and by making sure that clashing personalities don't find themselves being forced to work together.

Research suggests that humans are as territorial as any other animal. Watch people getting on the morning train. The same people will sit in the same seats day after day. The same goes for office supplies. How many times have you picked up a stapler in the office and found its owner's name written in large letters? A stapler!

Do you know how much time team members spend protecting their territory?

What is the team's territory?

Let me give an example of how territorial behavior can make even a minor incident into a major one. During a series of one-on-one employee interviews I conducted I met with an administrative assistant whose biggest complaint was that she had to go to the supply room every Monday morning to get herself new pens. She always took a full box, but by the end of the week everyone else in the office would have helped themselves to her pens. It seemed to her that everyone had nothing better to do than stop by her desk and leave with a pen. Small incidents like this one might actually lead to big problems.

Distance

We like to keep our loved ones approximately within two feet of us. We do a lot to keep others farther away. Of course, that's not realistic on the bus or the subway during rush hour. If you watch people in that sort of situation, you'll see how uncomfortable they feel. They look away, and often they'll use newspapers or bags as a barrier. Humans do have the need to keep a certain amount of distance between themselves and others. You can see this with cars; look how large they've gotten in the past decade.

The closer you are to someone the more intimate the relationship usually is. You can see this when you watch people who work together; judging from the distance between two co-workers you can usually tell whether they're friends, enemies, or just two people who work together.

Between two and four feet is the distance we keep with good friends and people we know. That's our personal area. Turning around and or looking at the other is usually seen as a sign we want to chat.

Between four feet and two yards is the *social zone*. That's where you keep your co-workers, your boss, and acquaintances. Some businesses create this distance with furniture to keep this distance between their employees and the customers—banks are a perfect example. Police officers (or your drill sergeant), on the other hand, will always get into your intimate zone when they think you did something wrong. So might an angry manager. This makes the person being confronted extremely uncomfortable!

Once the distance is above the social zone we are talking about the *public distance*. That's the distance you usually reserve for people you do not know, such as patrons in the library. Here's an easy experiment you can conduct: take the time to go to the movies early. Sit in the last rows so you can observe how people choose to sit where they do, and how much distance they try to maintain.

No matter what the distance, people are always receptive to what they see as a pleasant demeanor—in other words, a smiling face.

Did you know that you can recognize a smile as far as 50 yards away?

Do you now understand the saying "A smile goes a long way"?
When did you last smile at your team?

Terrain

Distance is always with you, but your terrain is usually static—your home, your office. Protection is part of that territorial instinct. Do you lock your house or your car all the time? Or do you live in one of those neighborhoods where everyone trusts everyone else?

"Home sweet home"

Just look at the different kind of rituals employees go through when they come to work. Some have the odd habit of playing with things they find on others' desks. Do you think they have ever considered that an intrusion of the others territory? How about the people who sit at those desks?

How often do you violate someone's territory?

Does every team member have enough distance to others?

Cubicles or Just Stables?

A company decided to move its offices—while in the middle of a large-scale project. If you've ever moved a business, you know that it requires way more work than moving one's home, because the workflow has to be seamless while the move is going on. So moving during a complicated project like this company was what many people would call insane. Well, knowing the difficult time constraints everyone was up against, management came up with what they called a "bright idea." Employees working on that project were not allowed to perform moving tasks during their normal working hours. The majority of the workers were clocking in well above 50 hours a week. Some as much as 80 hours a week.

For some this was the first time they even knew they were supposed to be helping move the office! Staffers who telecommuted and worked part-time in the office complained that they shouldn't have to come in to help move. Management agreed—shifting responsibility on everyone else.

By now you know it got worse. Imagine the employees' surprise when they first saw the new space: one huge open space with everyone but management side by side with the help desk. Cubicle walls barely reached the monitors on the desks. One regulator for air conditioning and heat—and *one light switch* for the whole space. Especially hard on those who are very picky about their work space. How would you feel in a work environment like that? How would anyone feel?

Anyway, here's what one of those workers had to say about the new space: *"By the way, I think that calling them cubicles is completely wrong.*

I am calling them stables. For obvious reasons. Your shelves are actually higher than the stable walls. The good thing about the stables, from a management point of view, is that you can see if the livestock is all in the proper stables at the proper time. I think my desk is the ONLY one that you have to take more than a few steps to see since it is located around the corner.

Privacy? Of course not!

Plus they can easily check if we actually do the work they think we should do."

This reminds me of the design department at a large manufacturing firm. One day a vice president walked through and spotted one of the engineers sitting at his desk, feet propped up, just staring at the ceiling. Five minutes later the VP returned to check the engineer out; sure enough, he was still doing nothing. The VP went to the department manager to complain. "Just what is it that he's supposed to be doing?" he asked. Said the manager: *"He thinks."*

How would you feel at work if you knew that every few minutes someone would either peer over your walls or walk by your cubicle? One of the biggest complaints of people who work in cubicles is that the walls don't filter out noise because they're not tall enough. People can hear their co-workers' conversations, phone calls, and music (if anyone is bold enough to turn on a radio).

In one company, employees asked for cubicle walls. Management refused, and morale deteriorated. People don't want to feel like fish in a fishbowl. Yet, the fix would have been so easy: remember one of the sins at the beginning of the book? Exactly! *Listen to your employees!* And don't create stables! If you really have to go with cubicles let them have high enough walls to give the employees enough privacy. And educate your people to show consideration for others.

Does your team feel comfortable in the provided working space?

Does the team have the ability to communicate fast and easy?

Without disturbing others?

Manners

Are manners and management a strange combination? Of course not—although in some companies you wouldn't realize it. The truth is that well-mannered people are more readily accepted than those with poor manners. The rules of etiquette may be slightly different from country to country, but politeness is always a recognized and welcome attribute. A study of 600 managers conducted by Munich CGC Claus Goworr Consulting showed that 87 percent see a direct connection between good manners and personal success. Three out of four think that manners influence the outcome of negotiations.

The ancient Romans said that youth has no manners— so the perception of lack of manners is clearly nothing new. But what are manners really? Most people have a slightly different understanding of manners. Manners rules how you eat, greet, talk and date. But those rules change with different cultures and different areas. Manners are learned from the parents and then refined during one's lifetime. Sometimes the rules change slightly because of the situation: just think about how you greet your boss, and how you greet a close friend.

Most people consider respectful, thoughtful and helpful behavior toward others to be good manners—along with language (something as simple as "thank you" and "please"). Good manners help you to make the right impression within the first few seconds of meeting someone. People usually are more open and more helpful when you display good manners.

Do you know the right manners to overcome first time situations?

Are you working on your manners?

> *"The hardest job kids face today is learning good
> manners without seeing any."*
> *Fred Astaire*

Don't make the mistake of thinking that manners are a sign of phoniness. If your good manners aren't genuine—if you don't make a sincere effort to be helpful and pleasant—people will know. Good manners are important to anyone who wants to climb the corporate ladder because good manners tell others that a person is decent, caring, and reasonable.

Do your clothes send out the wrong message?

Are you talking yourself out of it?

Are your manners a killer?

Can you distinguish between "New York", "Smart", and "Business Casual"?

And what about "Casual", "Informal", and "Business Attire"?

Cultural Differences

Just because you disagree with someone, or you don't understand someone's point of view, it doesn't mean that person is wrong or in need of mentoring.

"Our greatest strength as a human race is our ability to acknowledge our differences, our greatest weakness is our failure to embrace them."
Judith Henderson

To some Europeans, people who don't make direct eye contact are thought to be ignoring them. West Africans, on the other hand, consider direct eye contact a sign of aggression. It's easy to see how different views of cultural cues can be confusing and inadvertently insulting.

Did you know that for cats waving the tail is aggression, while for dogs…?

"Culture" is one of the most misunderstood words. The rules you have learned and grown up with change the moment you leave your hometown. And because everything has become part of your nature, often it's hard to judge how different things have become.

A great many still think that "culture" is something like theater, opera, and museums. But culture is everything we as humans are made of. There is no right or wrong culture—just *different* ones.

Are you tolerant toward other cultures?

Do you respect their diversity?

There will always be times when we don't understand the reasoning behind the actions of someone from another cultural background. But as long as we understand that different cultures have different ways of doing things, we can usually work together reasonably well.

Companies entering a new market in a different culture that they don't understand are likely to fail if they haven't done their research. Ignorance and prejudices are only part of the problem. A leading manufacturer lost big in sales when management did not care that the name of the product they tried to sell had the meaning of a vulgar term to the potential customers in one market.

> *"Any communication or marketing professional*
> *needs cross-cultural research and communication*
> *skills to be able to succeed in the future."*
> *Marye Tharp*

Step 7

Bring the Fun to Work

Fun?

Unfortunately, too many seem to think that fun at work is a must-do, an obligation. This of course defeats the whole purpose of fun. In fact, when fun is seen as a requirement, any motivational value is lost—because employees can actually come to dislike fun.

Teams need to understand that having fun should never be a requirement but rather a desired side effect. Often, employers simply add "having fun" to the list of things employees need to do during the day. It becomes nothing more than just another thing to get done. Result: there's less genuine fun, but plenty more frustration.

Let's not forget that historically, fun and work haven't exactly been best buddies. We should always try to make employees feel more fulfilled in doing and enjoying their work. If you're going to implement "fun," it needs to be done with the same care as any other strategic management tool.

Remember also that for many people, "fun" isn't clowning around and telling jokes. Sometimes just the work itself can be fun. There's a story about a young Japanese man who opened an auto repair shop. He really got enjoyment out of working on cars—to him, it was fun. The business grew and he hired mechanics, but he drew the line at opening more shops. "Think of all the extra money you'll make," his friends and family said. But he modestly declined, explaining, "Once I do that, I won't be having any fun anymore."

A study of IT workers (yes, IT workers) revealed that 70 percent of them see fun at work as the number one priority. And 98 percent of 700 interviewed CEOs said they prefer to hire an employee with a sense of humor. In some workplaces it seems as though the opposite is true. Someone ought to tell all those grouches that it takes fewer muscles to smile.

Many studies have shown that as many as one third of all employees consider fun to be an important part of the corporate culture. Humor is important to help people to loosen up; to become more creative. It has nothing to do with avoiding work or even working less efficiently. Can you imagine a ball game without the winning players celebrating and joking around? And there's a reason so many movie DVDs include outtakes that include all the bloopers that had to be cut from the film. Fun is—well, fun!

Think the actors had fun while working?

"Humor is when you laugh anyway."
German proverb

Basically there are two teaching strategies that get people to retain what they learn:
   Fun
   Parable
When was the last time you sat through a training session and got either of those? Doesn't happen too often, now does it?

When was the last time the team had fun?

Laughed together?

Created something outstanding while having fun?

Worked out a stuck situation with a smile?

Continued to be mad with someone who smiled at them?

How can we add fun?
1. Start with yourself
2. Never force it
3. Inspire others
4. Allow fun
5. Make fun part of the job
6. Find the positive in every situation
7. Smile, smile, smile

Some years ago I hold a session for a team of engineers on the rather dry topic of assembly. My session was one in many over the course of three days. I guarantee you that every one of those engineers remembers my session. Why? Because I managed to make it funny. You can teach anyone anything—as long as you can generate interest. People who have fun at work actually work more productively. Which store do you prefer to go shopping at—the one with the grumpy employees or the one where people genuinely smile at you and make you feel good?

Think about hobbies. Did one of your hobbies ever burn you out? Did you ever consider getting out of your hobby? Many dot-com bombs succeeded early on because they were able to motivate employees by creating a fun work environment. Now, to be fair, some of those companies might have taken fun a bit too far (or profits not far enough!)—but you rarely hear former dot-com employees complain that they didn't enjoy their jobs.

So why aren't there more companies requiring the work environment to be more of a joy? Look around you—are those managers just too inflexible or are they not willing to go the extra mile to try something new and fail at times?

Burn-Outs

Burned out employees tend to be depressed—and they're usually make those around them depressed, too. They can easily change the mood of everyone around them. A dangerous chain-reaction starts that can destroy even the best team.

The typical burn-out runs through six different phases:
1. increased engagement in work, tendency to make themselves irreplaceable
2. decreased engagement in work, negative attitude toward work and co-workers
3. playing the blame game, depression, aggression
4. loss of creativity, motivation, and efficiency
5. becoming mentally, socially, and emotionally withdrawn
6. insomnia, deep depression, stomach problems

Do you live to work or work to live?

Appendix

The Fun Standard[9]

Document number: 37IWS-SMILE
Date effective: Today
Owner: Everyone

1. Purpose

There are standards to describe all sorts of processes in all kinds of organizations all over the world. These processes preserve best practices and prevent the wasteful reinvention of excellence, but they can't create success by themselves. People must also enjoy their work to be productive.

Maximum productivity is obtained by having fun. This standard collects activities that help organizations have fun. Addition of the final ingredient, the actual "fun" itself, can only be done by you.

2. Definition

Fun: Consisting of animation, bliss, buoyancy, cheer, chuckles, delight, gladness, happiness, jests, jokes, joviality, joy, laughter, light-heartedness, merriment, mirth, play, pleasantries, quips, rapture, sport, tranquility, and witticism.

---

[9] Unrestricted permission granted to copy, distribute, modify, improve, or reuse in any form. V20050405
The latest version can always be found at http://LivingInternet.com/fun/

3. Process

The organization shall be predisposed to mutual cooperation, trust, communication, and goodwill.

3.1 Management will:

- View themselves as employees of their organization, and focus on removing roadblocks and providing the resources their staff needs to perform their work.
- Improve the plan, manage the schedule, put the right people in the right place, and ensure that everyone knows how they can help the team.
- Have at least one meeting a week, mandate attendance at no more than 2 hours of regular meetings a week, hold regular meetings in the afternoon, and start every meeting with a statement of its purpose.
- Practice management by walking around (MBWA) to obtain unfiltered information about how the organization functions.
- Make promotions on merit, plus demonstration that at least one member of their staff can do their job as well as they can.
- Assign responsibility, authority, and accountability as a single package.
- Praise in public, criticize in private.
- Schedule based on bottom-up estimates prepared by people who perform the work, and plan to minimize overtime.
- Ensure that no staff member needs more than 15 minutes a week to prepare regular reports.
- Provide a feedback mechanism for employees to communicate with top management, and visibly action and reward useful suggestions.
- Share profits with everyone in the organization.
- Share credit for all successes, and take responsibility for all failures.

3.2 Employees will:

- Place first priority on fulfillment of the goals of the whole organization, and refrain from construction of disconnected empires unrelated to business goals.

- Never ask for something they don't need, never promise results they know can't be delivered, do anything they say they'll do, and provide notification as far in advance as possible when circumstances prevent fulfillment of a commitment.
- Share information with everyone, never use technical double-talk, and say they don't know when they don't know.
- Maintain a good working relationship with all departments, and respect all personnel independent of their area of expertise.
- Decrease the complexity and shorten the cycle times of all processes under their control.
- Write documents to be read; use brevity to maximize clarity.
- Double-check anything they give to others for accuracy, completeness, and consistency.
- Relate to their boss the way they would like employees to relate to them if they were the boss.

3.3 Human Resources will:

- Ensure that all personnel receive at least three weeks of vacation a year, and that at least three weeks of unused vacation can be carried over from one year to the next.
- Facilitate flexible working hours, and allow overtime hours worked to be taken in time off.
- Provide all personnel with medical, dental, and disability insurance, and repay out-of-pocket expenses within two weeks.
- Ensure that all personnel receive at least one week of training a year, and enable employees to choose their own training if not chosen by their management.
- Ensure that jerks and meanies are counseled, and, if unresponsive, allocated to a peripheral group where they can't damage the rest of the organization and have to work exclusively with each other until reformed.

3.4 Facilities will:

- Ensure that at least three live plants and one outside window are

visible from every working area.
- Reduce, absorb, and deflect noise wherever possible.
- Use only full spectrum lighting.
- Ensure that bathroom stalls are at least three feet wide, toilet paper has a roughness level less than plywood, water taps stay open for at least five seconds, and at least one shower is available.
- Make printable whiteboards and markers in at least three colors available to all staff.
- Provide all personnel with a computer no more than three years old, with word processing, spreadsheet, database, and graphics applications, and email, newsgroup, and web access.

3.5 All Personnel will:

- Strive for excellence through continuous improvement in all aspects of their job.
- Actively listen to everyone, never interrupt, and change their mind when they hear a better idea.
- Be gender, disability, religion, and color blind, respect all personnel as human beings of equal value, and never try to increase their sense of self-esteem by decreasing someone else's.
- Never spread harmful gossip about others, and congratulate others whenever possible with specifics.
- Turn complaints into constructive suggestions for improvement.
- Protect the environment and save costs at the same time.
- Never come to work with a contagious or infectious illness.
- Erase the whiteboard at the end of the meeting.
- Take coffee from the second pot, and make a new pot when the second pot is empty.
- Never raise their voice, keep a sense of humor, and smile at least twice a day for at least five seconds each time.

4. Exit Criteria

This process ends when all personnel look forward to coming to work at the start of each day, and leave at the end of each day with a genuine sense of joy, self-worth, and achievement.

Failure to have fun will not be tolerated.

This version supersedes previous issues and takes precedence over constitutions.

5. References

The following references are applicable to this document.

a. Scott Adams, "The Dilbert Principle".

b. Norman Augustine, "Augustine's Laws".

c. David Firth, "How To Make Work Fun".

d. C. Northcote Parkinson, "The Law".

e. Robert Townsend, "Up The Organization".

Bibliography

Al Ries, Jack Trout; *Horse Sense: The Key to Success Is Finding a Horse to Ride* (McGraw-Hill, 1990)

Alan Lakein; *How to Get Control of Your Time and Your Life* (Signet Book, 1996)

Andrew Hargadon; *How Breakthroughs Happen: The Surprising Truth About How Companies Innovate* (Harvard Business School Press, 2003)

Anthony Robbins; *Awaken the Giant Within: How to Take Immediate Control of Your Mental, Emotional, Physical, and Financial* (Free Press 1992)

Barbara Kellerman; *Bad Leadership: What It Is, How It Happens, Why It Matters (Leadership for the Common Good)* (Harvard Business School Press, 2004)

Bryan Dodge, David Cottrell; *Becoming the Obvious Choice* (Cornerstone Leadership Inst, 2001)

Carl Sewell, Paul B. Brown; *Customers For Life: How To Turn That One-Time Buyer Into a Lifetime Customer* (Currency, 2002)

Clayton M. Christensen; *The Innovator's Dilemma* (Collins, 2003)

Clayton M. Christensen, Erik A. Roth, Scott D. Anthony; *Seeing What's Next: Using Theories of Innovation to Predict Industry Change* (Harvard Business School Press, 2004)

Clayton M. Christensen, Michael E. Raynor; *The Innovator's Solution: Creating and Sustaining Successful Growth* (Harvard Business School Press, 2003)

Cynthia D., Ph.D. Scott, Dennis, Ph.D. Jaffe, Dennis T. Jaffe; *Managing Change at Work: Leading People Through Organizational Transitions* (Crisp Learning, 2004)

Dale Carnegie; *How to Win Friends & Influence People* (Pocket, 1990)

Daniel Goleman; *Emotional Intelligence: Why It Can Matter More Than IQ* (Bantam, 1997)

Daniel Goleman; *Working with Emotional Intelligence* (Bantam, 1998)

Daniel Goleman, Michael MacCoby, Thomas Davenport, John C. Beck, Dan Clampa, Michael Watkins; *Harvard Business Review on What Makes a Leader* (Harvard Business School Press, 2001)

Daniel Goleman, Richard Boyatzis, Annie McKee; *Primal Leadership: Learning to Lead with Emotional Intelligence* (Harvard Business School Press, 2004)

Daniel Goleman, William Peace, William Pagonis, Tom Peters, Gareth Jones, Harris Collingwood; *Harvard Business Review on Breakthrough Leadership* (Harvard Business School Press, 2002)

Danny Miller, Isabelle Le Breton-Miller; *Managing For The Long Run: Lessons In Competitive Advantage From Great Family Businesses* (Harvard Business School Press, 2005)

Daniel Pink; *A Whole New Mind: Moving from the Information Age to the Conceptual Age* (Riverhead Hardcover, 2005)

David Schwartz; *The Magic of Thinking Big* (Fireside, 1987)

Denis Waitley; *Seeds Of Greatness* (Pocket, 1988)

Dennis Romig; *Side by Side Leadership: Achieving Outstanding Results Together* (Bard Press, 2001)

Donald T. Phillips; *The Founding Fathers on Leadership: Classic Teamwork in Changing Times* (Warner Books, 1998)

Edward De Bono; *Lateral Thinking: Creativity Step by Step* (Harper Paperbacks, 1973)

Eliyahu M. Goldratt, Jeff Cox; *The Goal: A Process of Ongoing Improvement* (North River Press, 1992)

Erik Weihenmayer; *Touch the Top of the World: A Blind Man's Journey to Climb Farther than the Eye Can See: My Story* (Plume, 2002)

Frank M.J. LaFasto, Carl E. Larson; *When Teams Work Best: 6,000 Team Members and Leaders Tell What It Takes to Succeed* (SAGE Publications, 2001)

Frans Johansson; *The Medici Effect: Breakthrough Insights at the Intersection of Ideas, Concepts, and Cultures* (Harvard Business School Press, 2004)

George Stalk, Rob Lachenauer, John Butman; *Hardball: Are You Playing to Play or Playing to Win* (Harvard Business School Press, 2004)

Gerard Nierenberg; *How to Read a Person Like a Book* (Pocket, 1990)

Harvey Mackay; *Dig Your Well Before You're Thirsty: The Only Networking Book You'll Ever Need* (Currency, 1999)

Harvey MacKay; *Pushing the Envelope All the Way to the Top* (Ballantine Books, 2000)

Harvey Mackay; *Swim with the Sharks Without Being Eaten Alive: Outsell, Outmanage, Outmotivate, and Outnegotiate Your Competition* (Ballantine Books, 1996)

Heike Bruch, Sumantra Ghoshal; *A Bias for Action: How Effective Managers Harness Their Willpower, Achieve Results, and Stop Wasting Time* (Harvard Business School Press, 2004)

Henry Mintzberg; *Managers Not MBAs: A Hard Look at the Soft Practice of Managing and Management Development* (Berrett-Koehler Publishers, 2004)

Henry Mintzberg, John Kotter, Abraham Zaleznik, Joseph Badaracco, Charles Farkas, Ronald Heifetz, Donald Laurie; *Harvard Business Review on Leadership* (Harvard Business School Press, 1998)

Hermann Simon; *Hidden Champions: Lessons from 500 of the World's Best Unknown Companies* (Harvard Business School Press, 1996)

Howard Gardner; *Changing Minds: The Art and Science of Changing Our Own and Other People's Minds* (Harvard Business School Press, 2004)

Ivan R. Misner, Don Morgan; *Masters of Success* (Entrepreneur Press, 2004)

J. Richard Hackman; *Leading Teams: Setting the Stage for Great Performances* (Harvard Business School Press, 2002)

J. Richard Hackman (Editor); *Groups That Work (and Those That Don't): Creating Conditions for Effective Teamwork* (Jossey-Bass, 1989)

Jack D. Wilner; *Seven Secrets to Successful Sales Management: The Sales Manager's Manual* (CRC Press, 1997)

Jack Welch, Suzy Welch; *Winning* (Collins, 2005)

James M. Burns; *Leadership* (Harper Perennial, 1982)

James M. Kouzes, Barry Z. Posner; *The Leadership Challenge* (Jossey-Bass, 2003)

Jean Lipman-Blumen; *The Allure Of Toxic Leaders: Why We Follow Destructive Bosses And Corrupt Politicians—and How We Can Survive Them* (Oxford University Press, 2004)

Jerry Wisinski; *Building a Partnership With Your Boss: A Take-Charge Assistant Book* (American Management Association, 1999)

Jim Collins; *Good to Great: Why Some Companies Make the Leap... and Others Don't* (Collins, 2001)

Jim Collins, Jerry I. Porras; *Built to Last: Successful Habits of Visionary Companies* (Collins, 2002)

John Antonakis (Editor), Anna T. Cianciolo (Editor), Robert J. Sternberg (Editor); *The Nature of Leadership* (SAGE Publications, 2004)

John C. Maxwell, Zig Ziglar; *The 21 Irrefutable Laws of Leadership* (Nelson Business, 1998)

John Cotter, James Heskett; *Corporate Culture and Performance* (Free Press, 1992)

John P. Kotter, James Collins, Richard Pascale, Jeanie Daniel Duck, Jerry Porras, Anthony Athos; *Harvard Business Review on Change* (Harvard Business School Press, 1998)

John S. Hammond, Ralph L. Keeney, Howard Raiffa; *Smart Choices: A Practical Guide to Making Better Decisions* (Broadway, 2002)

John T. Molloy; *Molloy's Live for Success* (William Morrow & Co, 1981)

John W. Gardner; *On Leadership* (Free Press, 1993)

Jon R. Katzenbach, Douglas K. Smith; *The Wisdom of Teams: Creating the High-Performance Organization* (Collins, 2003)

Jon R. Katzenbach, Douglas K. Smith; *The Discipline of Teams: A Mindbook-Workbook for Delivering Small Group Performance* (Wiley, 2001)

Joseph L. Badaracco Jr.; *Defining Moments: When Managers Must Choose Between Right and Right* (Harvard Business School Press, 1997)

Joseph L. Badaracco Jr.; *Leading Quietly* (Harvard Business School Press, 2002)

Karl Von Clausewitz; *On War* (Penguin Books, 1982)

Ken Blanchard; *Gung Ho! Turn On the People in Any Organization* (William Morrow, 1997)

Ken Blanchard, Mark Miller; *The Secret: What Great Leaders Know—And Do* (Berrett-Koehler Publishers, 2004)

Ken Blanchard, Patricia Zigarmi; *Leadership and the One Minute Manager: Increasing Effectiveness Through Situational Leadership* (William Morrow, 1999)

Ken Blanchard, Sheldon Bowles; *High Five! The Magic of Working Together* (William Morrow, 2001)

Ken Blanchard, Spencer Johnson; *The One Minute Manager* (William Morrow, 1982)

Larry Bossidy, Ram Charan; *Confronting Reality: Doing What Matters to Get Things Right* (Crown Business, 2004)

Larry Bossidy, Ram Charan, Charles Burck; *Execution: The Discipline of Getting Things Done* (Crown Business, 2002)

Malcolm Gladwell; *Blink: The Power of Thinking Without Thinking* (Little, Brown, 2005)

Malcolm Gladwell; *The Tipping Point: How Little Things Can Make a Big Difference* (Back Bay Books, 2002)

Marcus Buckingham; *The One Thing You Need to Know: ... About Great Managing, Great Leading, and Sustained Individual Success* (Free Press, 2005)

Marcus Buckingham, Curt Coffman; *First, Break All the Rules: What the World's Greatest Managers Do Differently* (Simon & Schuster, 1999)

Mark Amtower; *Government Marketing Best Practices: Real World Tactics On How To Grow Mindshare And Increace Marketshare To Grab A Bigger Slice Of The World's Largest Market—"Fortune One"* - The U.S. F (Amtower & Company, 2005)

Mark H. McCormack; *What They Don't Teach You At Harvard Business School: Notes From A Street-Smart Executive* (Bantam, 1986)

Mark H. McCormack; *What They Still Don't Teach You At Harvard Business School* (Bantam, 1990)

Martin Linsky, Ronald A. Heifetz; *Leadership on the Line: Staying Alive Through the Dangers of Leading* (Harvard Business School Press, 2002)

Max H. Bazerman; *Negotiating Rationally* (Free Press, 1994)

Maxwell Maltz; *The Magic Power of Self-Image Psychology* (Pocket, 1983)

Michael Maccoby; *The Gamesman: The New Corporate Leaders* (Simon and Schuster, 1976)

Michael Maccoby; *The Leader: A New Face for American Management* (Ballantine Books, 1983)

Michael Maccoby; *The Productive Narcissist: The Promise and Peril of Visionary Leadership* (Broadway, 2003)

Michael Maccoby; *Why Work? Motivating the New Workforce* (Miles River Press, 1995)

Mike Krzyzewski (Author), Donald T. Phillips; *Leading with the Heart: Coach K's Successful Strategies for Basketball, Business, and Life* (Warner Business Books, 2001)

Miyamoto Musashi; *The Book of Five Rings* (Shambhala, 2000)

Nancy Austin, Thomas J Peters; *A Passion for Excellence: The Leadership Difference* (Warner Books, 1989)

Napoleon Hill; *Think and Grow Rich* (Aventine Press, 2004)

Norman V. Peale, Ken Blanchard; *The Power of Ethical Management* (William Morrow, 1988)

Nuala Beck; *Shifting Gears: Thriving in the New Economy* (Harpercollins Canada, 1993)

Patrick M. Lencioni; *Death by Meeting: A Leadership Fable...About Solving the Most Painful Problem in Business* (Jossey-Bass, 2004)

Patrick M. Lencioni; *The Five Dysfunctions of a Team: A Leadership Fable* (Jossey-Bass, 2002)

Patrick M. Lencioni; *The Five Temptations of a CEO: A Leadership Fable* (Jossey-Bass, 1998)

Patrick M. Lencioni; *The Four Obsessions of an Extraordinary Executive: A Leadership Fable* (Jossey-Bass, 2000)

Peter F. Drucker; *Managing for Results* (Collins, 1993)

Peter F. Drucker; *The Effective Executive Revised* (Collins, 2002)

Peter F. Drucker; *The Practice of Management* (Collins, 1993)

Peter Ferdinand Drucker, John Hammond, Ralph Keeney, Howard Raiffa, Alden M. Hayashi; *Harvard Business Review on Decision Making* (Harvard Business School Press, 2001)

Peter G. Northouse; *Leadership: Theory and Practice* (SAGE Publications, 2003)

Peter Urs Bender; *Leadership from Within* (The Achievement Group, 2002)

Ralph G. Nichols, Leonard A. Stevens, Fernando Bartolome, Chris Argyris; *Harvard Business Review on Effective Communication* (Harvard Business School Press, 1999)

Ram Charan; *Profitable Growth Is Everyone's Business: 10 Tools You Can Use Monday Morning* (Crown Business, 2004)

Ricardo Semler; *The Seven-Day Weekend: Changing the Way Work Works* (Portfolio Hardcover, 2004)

Richard Farson; *Management Of The Absurd* (Simon & Schuster, 1996)

Rick Pitino; *Lead to Succeed: 10 Traits of Great Leadership in Business and Life* (Broadway, 2001)

Rick Pitino; *Success Is a Choice* (Broadway, 1997)

Rita Gunther McGrath, Ian C. Macmillan; *MarketBusters: 40 Strategic Moves That Drive Exceptional Business Growth* (Harvard Business School Press, 2005)

Rob Goffee, Garetht Jones, Sterling Livingston, Pfeffe Jeffrey, David Thomas, Robin J. Ely, Jean-Frantois Manzoni, Jean-Louis Barsoux; *Harvard Business Review on Managing People* (Harvard Business School Press, 1999)

Robert B. Cialdini; *Influence: The Psychology of Persuasion* (Collins, 1998)

Roger E. Axtell (Editor); *Do's and Taboos Around The World (Do's and Taboos Around the World)* (Wiley, 1993)

Ron Chernow; *Titan: The Life of John D. Rockefeller, Sr.* (Vintage, 2004)

Ronald A. Heifetz; *Leadership Without Easy Answers* (Belknap Press September, 1994)

Rudolph W. Giuliani, Ken Kurson; *Leadership* (Miramax Books, 2002)

Rushworth M. Kidder; *How Good People Make Tough Choices: Resolving the Dilemmas of Ethical Living* (Harper Paperbacks, 2003)

Spencer Johnson; *Who moved my cheese?: An amazing way to deal with change in your work and in your life* (Vermilion, 1999)

Stephanie Winston; *The Organized Executive: A Program for Productivity—New Ways to Manage Time, Paper, People, and the Electronic Office*, (Warner Business Books, 2001)

Stephen E. Kohn, Vincent D. O'connell; *6 Habits of Highly Effective Bosses* (Career Press, 2005)

Stephen J. Hoch, Howard C. Kunreuther, Robert E. Gunther; *Wharton on Making Decisions* (Wiley, 2001)

Stephen R. Covey; *First Things First Every Day: Daily Reflections—Because Where*

You're Headed Is More Important Than How Fast You Get There (Fireside, 1997)

Stephen R. Covey; *Living The 7 Habits: The Courage To Change* (Simon & Schuster, 1999)

Stephen R. Covey; *Principle Centered Leadership* (Simon & Schuster, 1991)

Stephen R. Covey; *The 8th Habit: From Effectiveness to Greatness* (Free Press, 2004)

Steven Berglas; *Reclaiming the Fire: How Successful People Overcome Burnout* (Random House, 2001)

Steven K. Scott; *Simple Steps to Impossible Dreams: The 15 Power Secrets of the World's Most Successful People* (Simon & Schuster, 1998)

Sun Tzu; *The Art of War* (Dover Publications, 2002)

Tom Coens, Mary Jenkins; *Abolishing Performance Appraisals: Why They Backfire and What to Do Instead* (Berrett-Koehler Publishers 2002)

Tom Peters; *Leadership* (DK ADULT, 2005)

Tom Peters, Robert Waterman; *In Search of Excellence: Lessons from Americas Best Run Companies* (Warner Books, 1988)

Tom Rath, Donald O. Clifton; *How Full Is Your Bucket? Positive Strategies for Work and Life* (Gallup Press, 2004)

Tony Buzan; *Use Both Sides of Your Brain* (Plume Books, 1991)

Tony Buzan, Barry Buzan; *The Mind Map Book: How to Use Radiant Thinking to Maximize Your Brain's Untapped Potential* (Plume, 1996)

Vince Lombardi; *What It Takes to Be #1: Vince Lombardi on Leadership* (McGraw-Hill Companies, 2003)

W. Chan Kim, Renée Mauborgne; *Blue Ocean Strategy: How to Create Uncontested Market Space and Make Competition Irrelevant* (Harvard Business School Press, 2005)

Warren Bennis; *On Becoming A Leader: The Leadership Classic—Updated And Expanded* (Perseus Publishing, 2003)

Warren E. Buffett; *The Essays of Warren Buffett: Lessons for Corporate America* (The Cunningham Group, 2001)

Winston S. Churchill; *Never Give In: The Best of Winston Churchill's Speeches* (Hyperion, 2003)

Zig Ziglar; *See You at the Top* (Pelican Publishing Company, 2000)

Index

About The Author

Frank Kanu started out in sales before he decided to study computer science and later economics. As former CEO of three European corporations, Frank has gathered, refined, and implemented his management strategy—a strategy that has met with success.

Over the past two decades he has worked with a number of *Fortune* 500 companies to help managers improve success ratios and productivity levels. His client list includes IBM, Monster.com, AOL/Time Warner, Akzo Nobel, Crown Holdings, Inc., Raab Karcher Gruppe, and eon.

An award-winning speaker who enjoys sharing his insights with business leaders, Frank has lectured frequently and written articles for publications in the United States and Europe.

Besides spending his time with his lovely wife Ada and their three beautiful children, Frank enjoys skydiving, cycling and watching sports. He and Ada also love to cook and delight in surprising friends and acquaintances with their culinary skills.

LaVergne, TN USA
14 June 2010

186133LV00002B/12/A